The Dead Sea Scrolls
After Forty Years

On the cover: **View from a Qumran cave.** *In the second century B.C.E., a group of devout Jews, possibly Essenes, withdrew to this barren area adjacent to the Dead Sea, where they formed a community to await the end of an evil age. The remains of their settlement can be seen on the plateau. A library of more than 800 volumes, including all the books of the Hebrew Bible (except Esther) and documents delineating the sect's particular practices and beliefs, was stored, or hidden, in nearby caves.*
Biblical Archaeology Society/photo by Werner Braun

The
Dead Sea Scrolls
After Forty Years

Symposium at the Smithsonian Institution
October 27, 1990
Sponsored by the Resident Associate Program

HERSHEL SHANKS

JAMES C. VANDERKAM

P. KYLE McCARTER, JR.

JAMES A. SANDERS

BIBLICAL ARCHAEOLOGY SOCIETY
Washington, DC

Library of Congress Catalog Card Number: 91-71320
ISBN 0-9613089-7-4

Contents

List of Illustrations

List of Color Plates

Between pages 6-7

The Lecturers

 **Hershel Shanks** is founder, editor and publisher of *Biblical Archaeology Review* and *Bible Review*. He is the author of *The City of David* (Bazak, 1973), a guide to biblical Jerusalem; and *Judaism in Stone* (Harper & Row, 1979), tracing the development of ancient synagogues. He edited *Recent Archaeology in the Land of Israel* (Israel Exploration Society, 1984) with Professor Benjamin Mazar; *Ancient Israel: A Short History From Abraham to the Roman Destruction of the Temple* (Prentice Hall, 1988) and the two-volume *Archaeology and The Bible: The Best of Biblical Archaeology Review* (BAS, 1990). A graduate of Harvard Law School, he has also published widely on legal topics.

 **P. Kyle McCarter, Jr.,** is the William Foxwell Albright Professor of Biblical and Ancient Near Eastern Studies at the Johns Hopkins University in Baltimore, Maryland. Prior to going to Johns Hopkins in 1985, he taught for 11 years at the University of Virginia. His books and other publications include commentaries on 1 Samuel and 2 Samuel in the Anchor Bible series published by Doubleday. He is currently preparing a new edition and translation of the Copper Scroll from Qumran (3Q15) to be published by Princeton University Press.

James C. VanderKam, a professor of Old Testament at the University of Notre Dame, has written extensively on biblical languages and literature for a number of publications, including *Catholic Biblical Quarterly, Biblical Archaeologist, Journal of Biblical Literature* and *Bible Review*. He received a National Endowment for the Humanities Fellowship for 1989-1990 and is currently at work on a translation of a commentary on 1 Enoch 72-82 to appear in G. W. E. Nickelsburg's Hermeneia Commentary on 1 Enoch. He is also editing for publication the Qumran fragment from the Book of Jubilees.

James A. Sanders is professor of intertestamental and biblical studies at the School of Theology at Claremont, California, and professor of religion in the Claremont Graduate School. He is founder and president of the Ancient Biblical Manuscript Center for Preservation and Research, where he has developed an archive of thousands of biblical manuscripts on negatives, including all the Dead Sea Scrolls. He serves as associate editor of the Hebrew Old Testament Text Project of the United Bible Societies. His numerous publications include *The Dead Sea Psalms Scroll* (Cornell, 1967), *Torah and Canon* (Fortress Press, 1972), *Canon and Community: A Guide to Canonical Criticism* (Fortress Press, 1984) and *From Sacred Story to Sacred Text* (Fortress Press, 1987). He is also the editor of *Discoveries in the Judaean Desert IV: The Psalms Scroll of Qumran Cave 11* (Clarendon Press, 1965).

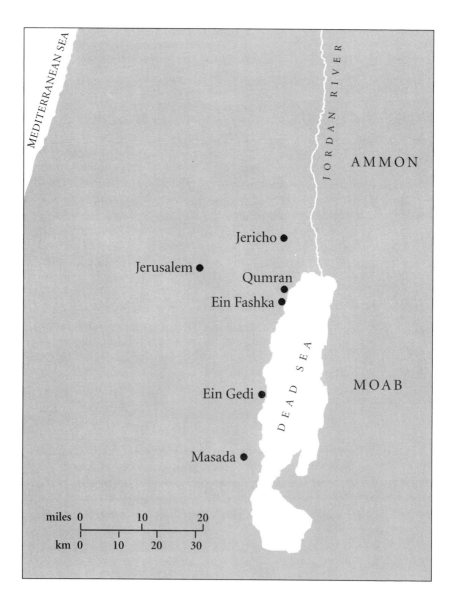

HERSHEL SHANKS

The Excitement Lasts

An Overview

T HIS IS A PICTURE OF A RARE wild orchid—a Showy Lady Slipper [color plate I]. In the United States, east of the Mississippi, there is only one place that it grows. The place is kept secret by the few people who know about it because if it became known, nothing would be there anymore. The next picture gives you a longer view. As you can see, in this one bog there are thousands of rare Showy Lady Slippers.

At this point you may be wondering whether I have gotten the wrong auditorium, the wrong lecture or the wrong date. No, I have a point to make. Even though the Showy Lady Slipper is very rare and grows in only one place, in fact, when you find it, there are thousands of them in that one place. And it is the same thing with the Dead Sea Scrolls. Even though they are very rare, once you find one you may find many, many others in approximately the same place.

And that is what happened with the Dead Sea Scrolls. The first point I want to impress upon you is that the Dead Sea Scrolls are an entire library. They include over 800 volumes. Can you imagine how rare and important a library of 800 volumes was 2,000 years ago? And what a remarkable thing it is to recover it 2,000 years after it was lost.

These books were stashed away in nearly inaccessible caves in the Judean wilderness.

I am going to give you an overview of the subject and then we will hear from three experts, each of whom has actually handled and deciphered some of the original scroll material.

Before we look at the scrolls themselves, let's look at the area where they were found. This picture shows the Qumran area [color plate II], where the scrolls were found. The deep valley is called the Wadi Qumran. A wadi is simply a dry riverbed that flows perhaps once or twice a year. If you happen to be there when that happens, it's very dangerous. You can easily drown in the sudden flood, it has such terrible force. But otherwise the riverbed is dry, as you can see in the picture. This wadi is located on the northwest shore of the Dead Sea, and the picture gives you some idea of the kind of terrain we are talking about. The scrolls were actually found in the caves above the valley. Sitting up on the plateau above the wadi are the remains of a settlement. The first question you'll ask is, what is the relationship of the settlement to the scrolls? That will introduce something we are going to have to face repeatedly today—that there are more questions than there are answers—and there are a lot of differences among scholars with respect to the answers we do have. One of the matters that is uncertain is the relationship of the Qumran settlement to the scrolls that were found in the Qumran caves.

The settlement was excavated in the 1950s, not long after the first of the scrolls were found in 1947. Unfortunately, the final report on this excavation has never been written, so there is much we don't know about the settlement. But there are some things we do know. In the middle of the settlement is the earliest cistern at the site, where water was stored. It is surrounded by a kitchen and a number of service buildings. In a long narrow room two inkwells were found and, in addition, some chairs or desks (at first they were thought to be desks, but they were probably chairs). Because of the inkwells and the possibility that these were desks on which something was written, that narrow room was denominated the scriptorium. It was assumed that there was a second floor where the scrolls were written. But this is another uncertain question.

Is it really likely that 800 scrolls were written in this settlement, even if it had a scriptorium?

Next to the so-called scriptorium is a long room that is supposed to be the dining room, because in the little room next to it over 1,000 eating vessels were found. The entire site has been interpreted by its excavator Père Roland de Vaux as a kind of a monastery. But this, too, is now questioned. Scholars, as you may or may not know, are not above personal biases; de Vaux, who died in 1971, was a Dominican priest, so

Public buildings of the Qumran community. *In the small rooms on the right, the Qumran sect may have stored and studied the scrolls. At the far left, steps lead down to a cistern, perhaps used for ritual bathing. Nestled in the hills on the right are the Qumran caves.* Biblical Archaeology Society/photo by Garo Nalbandian

he naturally tended to interpret the site as a kind of a medieval monastery, or even like the convent in Jerusalem where he lived. Today many scholars are questioning his interpretations.

A long wall separates the settlement from the area beyond. In the area beyond, outside the settlement, were some burials. Initially it was assumed that the people in the "monastery" were Essenes, a Jewish sect of the turn of the era. Some references in the literature suggest that at least some Essenes were celibate (they did not marry). So the question arises as to whether this settlement of Essenes was a celibate settlement. The excavator's initial answer was yes. But included in the burials in the cemetery are some women—two or perhaps as many as four—and also a child. Well, what does that do to the theory that celibate Essenes lived here in this monastery? Maybe not much. Maybe these were the women who did the cooking. Or maybe this evidence destroys the theory that the people in the settlement (the men) were celibate.

In a closer view of the caves, we can see Cave 4 [color plate III]. This is a crucial cave. In it, over 15,000 text fragments were found, comprising over 500 different documents. So 500 of the library of 800 books were found in this one cave. But all were in fragments. Inside, the caves were not clean and neat and level. On the contrary, they were often very difficult to excavate in. In Cave 4 there were 6 feet of bat dung and dust deposited over 2,000 years that the Bedouin and the archaeologists had to wade through in the stifling heat in order to try to extricate the fragments.

The Wadi Qumran is in the Judean wilderness. Adjacent to the Dead Sea, we are in the Great Rift Valley that extends from Africa up through the Jordan Valley north of the Dead Sea. The Dead Sea is the lowest point on earth, 1,290 feet below sea level. Beyond the Dead Sea, which incidentally has no outlet, to the east is modern-day Jordan, the site of ancient Moab and Ammon. It is a wonderful place to commune with God if ever there was one.

A few of the scrolls, about ten or so, were beautifully preserved and largely intact, like the scrolls of the Book of Isaiah [color plate IV]. But most consist of a lot of tiny fragments. Anyone who can read Hebrew can read the Isaiah scroll. It is made of animal skin. Linen threads tie the pieces together. Sometimes you can see notes or corrections or an insertion above a line. In the Isaiah scroll four dots appear where we would expect to find the tetragrammaton, the four-letter Hebrew name of God, often pronounced Yahweh, which the scribe did not want to write—it was too holy.

The settlement at Qumran was full of water containers called cisterns. Whether they were for ritual baths or just ordinary cisterns for water collecting is another matter scholars argue about. Many scholars feel the sect that lived there was involved in ritual bathing. There are far too many water cisterns just to supply water for the group living there, so the supposition is that at least some cisterns were for ritual bathing. Sometimes the steps going down to a bath have a divider. This might be a repair after an earthquake, but another theory about the separations is that you go down one side impure and come up the other side having been purified in the water.

The first of the Dead Sea Scrolls was found in 1947,probably February, by some Bedouin shepherds.* While they were searching for lost sheep, one of these young boys took a stone and tossed it into a cave. That cave later became very famous as Cave 1, because when he tossed the stone into the cave, the boy heard a cracking sound. What he actually heard was the sound of a pottery vessel being broken. The next day the shepherds examined the cave where the pottery vessel had been broken and they found some scrolls in there. They did not know what they were. They were members of the Ta'amireh tribe of Bedouin

---

* See Harry Thomas Frank, "How the Dead Sea Scrolls Were Found," *Biblical Archaeology Review*, December 1975.

Steps to captured waters. *Whether for comfort, cleanliness, drinking or praying, we can't be certain, but it is certain that this stairway led to water. Plaster, sealing the porous rock, is still evident on the steps and wall at right. The Qumran settlement had many cisterns, or containers, for collecting water. Many scholars believe that the Qumran group practiced ritual bathing since there are far more cisterns than necessary simply to store water for domestic use. According to some scholars, these steps were repaired after an earthquake. Others theorize that the dividers served a ritual purpose: One entered the bath impure on one side of the divider and exited the bath on the other side, purified. The water was directed into the bath through the center channel.*
Biblical Archaeology Society/photo by James Fleming

and they took their find to Bethlehem.

Eventually the scrolls found their way into the hands of a cobbler nicknamed Kando, who also dealt in antiquities in the back of his shop. Kando has become very famous. He died only in the last couple of years. Eventually he had a fine souvenir and antiquities shop in Jerusalem. It is still there in the lobby of St. George's Hotel. At that time, however, Kando was not very knowledgeable and his connections were not so great, but he started finding ways to sell the scrolls.

Several months later, the scrolls were shown to scholars at the American School of Oriental Research in Jerusalem and to Professor E. L. Sukenik at Hebrew University. There were the usual questions about whether the scrolls were fakes and, if not, what the date of the documents was. The great American archaeologist William F. Albright saw a photograph of a fragment and recognized it by the handwriting as genuine and about 2,000 years old; he telegraphed his view back to Jerusalem. Others in Jerusalem claimed that they had recognized this even earlier.

The story of the negotiations and the acquisition of these early scrolls is filled with tension and drama.* There were seven scrolls in Cave 1. In November 1947 Sukenik, who was not only a leading scholar but also the father of the great Israeli archaeologist Yigael Yadin, wanted to acquire these scrolls for Hebrew University. He raised some money, even mortgaging his own home. At that time his son was the head of the Haganah, the underground shadow army of the Israeli government that was being formed. Jerusalem itself was under Arab siege. Sukenik told his son, the head of the army, that he wanted to go to Bethlehem to acquire the scrolls. He now had the money and thought he could make a deal. His son, however, told him not to do it; it was too dangerous; Bethlehem was an Arab city. But Sukenik did not listen to his son's advice. He disobeyed his son. He got a pass to go through the line to the Arab side of divided Jerusalem and he got on a bus to Bethlehem—he was the only Jew on the bus—and then he returned to Jerusalem.

The day he did this was the day before the United Nations, by a two-thirds vote, passed the resolution creating the Jewish state. On the trip back to Jerusalem he carried with him, in a brown paper wrapper, three of the seven scrolls. The next day the United Nations passed this resolution. It was almost messianic. At the same time, literally within a 24-hour period, the state of Israel was created and Hebrew University acquired a scroll of the prophet Isaiah that was 1,000 years older than anything that had been known up to that time.

The four scrolls that Sukenik did not obtain ended up in the hands of an Assyrian cleric, the Metropolitan Samuel. There were all kinds of unsuccessful negotiations for the sale of these scrolls. Eventually the Metropolitan took them to New York, hoping to dispose of them in America at a better price. This turned out not to be so easy. It is a question as to why it was so difficult to sell these scrolls; the answer may have something to do with the fact that his title was unclear to prospective American purchasers. So he ended up putting a classified ad in the *Wall Street Journal* for four old scrolls.

As luck—or as God—would have it, when that blind ad, hardly recognizable, appeared in the *Wall Street Journal*, years after the discovery of the scrolls and the creation of the state of Israel, Yigael Yadin was

---

* See Hershel Shanks, "Failure to Publish Dead Sea Scrolls Is Leitmotif of New York University Scroll Conference," *Biblical Archaeology Review*, September/October 1985; Shanks, "Yigael Yadin 1917-1984," *Biblical Archaeology Review*, September/October 1984.

COLOR PLATE I

A Showy Lady Slipper. *This rare wild orchid* (Cypripedium reginae) *grows in just one place east of the Mississippi. Yet, in this bog, kept secret by the few who know its whereabouts, thousands of rare Showy Lady Slippers grow.* Hershel Shanks

COLOR PLATE II

The rumpled landscape of Qumran. *A wadi, or dry riverbed, cuts through the wilderness northwest of the Dead Sea. In the isolated spur, in the center, foreground, overlooking the wadi at right, are some of the 11 Qumran caves where scrolls were discovered. In the archaeological remains at left we see a large round cistern and, above the cistern to the right, two long, narrow rooms. One was a communal dining room; a pantry with more than 1,000 eating vessels was found adjacent. The other long room has been dubbed the scriptorium because two inkwells were found in it. Some scholars have suggested that at least some of the scrolls in the caves were copied here.* Biblical Archaeology Society/photo by Sonia Halliday

COLOR PLATE III

Pocked cliffs, repositories for precious documents. *On the second spur from the left are Caves 4 and 5. Cave 4 yielded more than 15,000 text fragments, representing over 500 different documents—more than any other cave. They were excavated from 6 feet of bat dung and dust deposited over 2,000 years. Among these fragments was one from Jubilees (see p. 30) discussed in the lecture by James VanderKam.* Biblical Archaeology Society/photo by Sonia Halliday

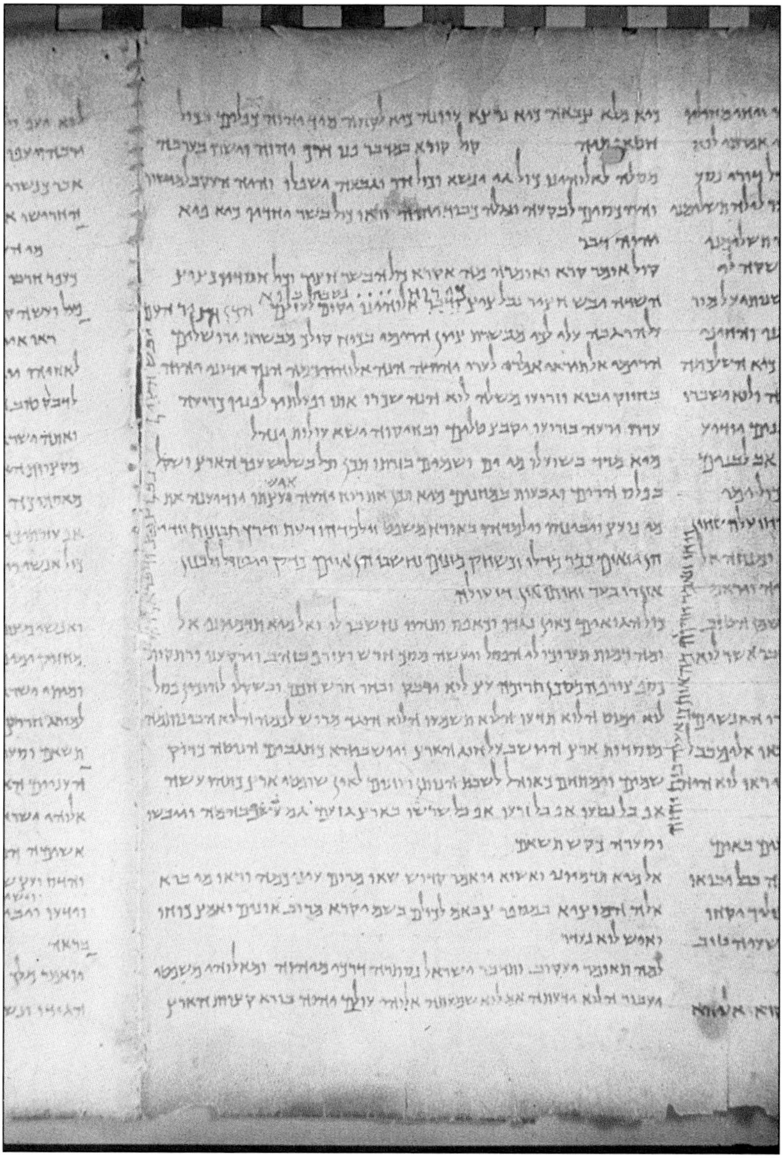

COLOR PLATE IV

The scroll of Isaiah. *Although many of the Qumran scrolls were found in fragments, some, like this Isaiah scroll, were largely intact. On the left side of the leather skin a linen thread ties two pieces together. Written in square, Aramaic Hebrew letters, similar to those used today, the scroll contains some scribal corrections and additions to the text along both margins and above the seventh line of text. In the insertion above line seven are four dots that serve as a substitute for the four-letter Hebrew name of Israel's God, yod heh vav heh, customarily spelled Yahweh in modern texts. This column of text (Isaiah 40:2-28) surely resonated for the religious sect that had retreated to the Judean wilderness: "In the wilderness prepare the way of the Lord" (Isaiah 40:3).* Biblical Archaeology Society/photo by John Trever

COLOR PLATE V

The illuminated carpet page from Leningradensis. *The text in the center of the star is a signature: "I am Samuel, the son of Jacob. I wrote the consonants and inserted the vowel points and the Masoretic notes."* Biblical Archaeology Society is grateful to Bruce and Kenneth Zuckerman of the West Semitic Research Project for allowing the reproduction of this photograph.

Inside a Qumran cave. *The first Dead Sea Scrolls were discovered by a Bedouin shepherd in 1947 when, while searching for lost sheep, he tossed a stone into a cave and heard a cracking sound. The cracking was the sound of pottery breaking. The arid atmosphere of the Judean wilderness preserved the ancient scrolls for two millennia.* Biblical Archaeology Society/photo by Richard Nowitz

in New York, and someone pointed out the ad to him. Yadin knew that the Metropolitan would not sell the scrolls to an Israeli, so Yadin used some fronts through whom he negotiated. When the final deal was struck and delivery was to be made, Yadin could not show up to examine the authenticity of the scrolls himself because the Metropolitan, Yadin feared, would back out. So Yadin called Professor Harry Orlinsky, whom many of you here know of, who lives today in Columbia, Maryland. Orlinsky was just leaving to go on a vacation. He came back into his house because he heard the phone ring. Yadin told him to come to New York; he couldn't tell him why, but it was very important. So Orlinsky changed his vacation plans and went to New York. Yadin told him that he was to be Mr. Green. He was to examine the scrolls for authenticity. This is a cloak-and-dagger business and it is very easy to get fooled; someone with Orlinsky's expertise was needed. So Orlinsky went to where they were being kept and identified himself as Mr. Green, looked at the scrolls and authenticated them.

That is how they were acquired for Israel for what was really a paltry sum, $250,000. That is how they went back to Israel. Some say that the Metropolitan must have known who he was selling them to because he was having such a tough time selling them to anyone who might be subject to a title-claim dispute. It was all just a show on the Metropolitan's part, so that he could claim he didn't know to whom he was selling them. Who knows? At any rate, the seven scrolls ended up in the Shrine of the Book, that beautiful museum in Israel shaped like the cover of one of the jars in which the scrolls were originally found.

Of course there was a scramble to find out where these scrolls came from. Eventually the cave was identified; the next thing was to see if there were other scrolls there or in nearby caves. In the years that followed, a little competition developed between the professional archaeologists and the Bedouin to find additional scroll material. The Bedouin almost always won. Most of the finds were made by the Bedouin. Eventually ten other caves with inscriptional material were discovered—a total of 11 Qumran caves. I say "inscriptional material" because in one of the caves there was only a ceramic ostracon. But in the others there were inscribed documents. The biggest find was in Cave 4. In Cave 4, there were over 500 of the 800 scrolls.*

The Cave 4 documents lie at the center of the publication problem, because it is that cache that remains largely unpublished today. In the 1950s, when this cave was discovered, the Qumran area was controlled by Jordan. The finds from Cave 4 were transferred to the Palestine Archaeological Museum, which is now called the Rockefeller. The thousands of fragments were put in a room dubbed the scrollery. A team of eight scholars—an international, interconfessional team—was put together with the help of various national schools under the auspices of the Jordanian government to edit and publish these texts.** The only rule that was imposed was that the group must be *Judenrein* (free of Jews). The people who were appointed, with one or two exceptions, were extremely competent men, conscientious, brilliant and certainly without prejudice,† but nevertheless they were bound by the restriction.

The seven intact scrolls from Cave 1 were promptly published by Israeli and American scholars. But the Cave 4 materials consisted of fragments only and presented a difficult problem. The fragments were all jumbled up. They had to be separated, they had to be organized. And it was the task of these scholars to do that. It took them until 1960 to arrange the fragments in plates, between sheets of glass. They tried to arrange them in terms of texts they could identify. Then they divvied

* See "Leading Dead Sea Scroll Scholar Denounces Delay," *Biblical Archaeology Review,* March/April 1990.

** See Frank Moore Cross, "Père de Vaux Was a Dead Sea Scroll Hero," *Biblical Archaeology Review,* Queries and Comments, January/February 1990.

† But see *Biblical Archaeology Review,* "Strugnell Denounces Judaism," January/February 1991, and "Silence, Anti-Semitism and the Scrolls," March/April 1991.

them up amongst themselves to publish. Today 80 percent of that cache remains secret and unpublished.

I will return to the publication problem, but first let me give you an overview of the kinds of documents found in the Qumran caves.* The 800 documents we call the Dead Sea Scrolls can be divided into several categories. The first category is the biblical texts. The oldest substantial copy of the Hebrew Bible that we knew of before the Qumran discoveries dated to about the tenth century C.E. Then along came Qumran, and now we have at least fragments of every book of the Hebrew Bible—except Esther—that are a thousand years older. Interestingly enough, Esther is the only book of the Hebrew Bible that does not mention the name of God and that is the one book that has not been found at Qumran.

The second category is what are called apocrypha and pseudepigrapha. We will consider them together. They are Bible-like books, often attributed to biblical heroes like Noah or Enoch. That is why they are called pseudepigrapha—they were written in somebody else's name. The apocrypha are some books that are not contained in the canon of the Hebrew Bible, but which are kind of supplemental, Bible-like books. These include Jubilees, which we are going to hear a lot about from Jim VanderKam; Enoch; the Testaments of the Twelve Patriarchs; and even an unpublished Book of Noah.

The third kind of text that we find at Qumran is called sectarian. This gets back to the problem of who these people were that produced these texts. At first there was a scholarly consensus that they were Essenes, a sect of Jews mentioned by Philo, the Alexandrian philosopher of the first century, and Josephus, the Jewish historian of the same period. We don't know much about the Essenes, but what we do know about them from these and a few other sources seems to be very much like what we know from these sectarian texts found at Qumran. There is a little circular reasoning involved in this and it's a bit dicey. Today you rarely hear scholars using the term "Essenes" with reference to the people who produced the sectarian texts that were found at Qumran. Instead, scholars talk about the Qumran sect, just to be safe. I remember asking one very eminent scholar, "Would you accept my referring to these texts as Essenic?" He replied, "Well, Essenoid."

Here is another problem: How do you tell which of these texts are sectarian and which are not? In any event, whoever these sectarians were, we have sectarian texts like the War Scroll, the Damascus Document and the Manual of Discipline, or Community Rule. These reflect a people who followed their version of sacred scripture very strictly; they

---

* See Frank Moore Cross, "The Dead Sea Scrolls and the People Who Wrote Them," *Biblical Archaeology Review*, March 1977.

had their own calendar (a solar calendar); they anticipated the immi-
nent end of days, or the Eschaton; at least one group lived a monastic-
like, celibate life, although some lived in cities as well. Sometimes it is
difficult to tell which of the documents are sectarian and which are not,
because there are many kinds of texts—hymns, psalms, prayers, a letter,
Bible commentaries, liturgical texts, a mezuzah (which Jews put on
their doorposts to this day), Targums (Aramaic translations or para-
phrases of biblical texts). All of these things are there, so the line between what is sectarian and what isn't is sometimes difficult to draw.
Sometimes clearly sectarian texts don't all fit together in their views.
They sometimes seem to contradict one another. That gets us into the
nature of the library as a whole—another very difficult problem.

I want to mention a couple of other kinds of texts. Most of these
texts are on leather. Most of them are in Hebrew, but a few are in
Aramaic and a few are in Greek. And on a shelflike space in the back of
Cave 3 was a very unusual document, unusual because it was written on
copper and rolled up. Can you imagine what kind of a document would
be written on copper sheet in those days, how important it must have
been? That document falls into a category of its own. It is called the
Copper Scroll. It was very difficult to unroll after 2,000 years. When it
was finally cut open, it was found to contain a kind of guide to a
treasure hunt—to the Temple treasures? We are going to hear more
about that from Kyle McCarter this afternoon. He will devote his entire
lecture to that so I won't steal his thunder.

Finally, the last scroll to be found was a very long one. It was 28 feet long.
It also involved Yigael Yadin.* In the early 1960s, out of the blue, someone who knew of Yadin's involvement with the scrolls sent him a fragment. Yadin died in 1984; during his lifetime no one but Yadin knew
who this man was who sent him this fragment. Yadin called him Mr. Z.
He did say he was a Virginia clergyman. When we printed this story in
the *Biblical Archaeology Review*, Mr. Z's wife happened to see the story,
and took it to her husband.** I can now tell you, Mr. Z was a man
named Joseph Uhrig who lived right out here in Virginia and who had a
connection with Kando in Bethlehem who still had scroll material.
Uhrig sent Yadin a little scrap Kando had given him which was a piece
of a psalm. Immediately Yadin recognized it, and he also recognized
that it came from a famous Psalm Scroll that was found in Cave 11. One
of the people we are going to hear from today is Jim Sanders, who was

* Yigael Yadin, "The Temple Scroll—The Longest and Most Recently Discovered Dead Sea Scroll," *Biblical Archaeology Review*, September/October 1984.

** Hershel Shanks, "Intrigue and the Scroll," *Biblical Archaeology Review*, November/December 1987.

the editor of that Psalm Scroll. Well, after Yadin made the deal for the little piece of the Psalm Scroll (and then gave it to Jim Sanders to publish), Uhrig said, "I have a big scroll."

To make a long story short, negotiations with Kando through Uhrig failed. Kando wanted a hundred thousand dollars for the scroll one day, the next day it was a million dollars, so they could not get together and negotiations were cut off. But Yadin knew that Kando had this scroll; he surmised it, although he was never told directly. After the Six-Day War in 1967, Bethlehem fell to the Israelis and the day after the war ended, Yadin went to Kando's house in Bethlehem with an army colonel and said he wanted the scroll. Kando knew the jig was up. He lifted a floorboard and underneath, in a shoe box, deteriorating terribly—parts of it were like chocolate—was this long scroll, now known as the Temple Scroll. The part that is preserved is 28 feet long. It is very well preserved and is easily readable. The character of the Qumran sect may turn on the relationship of this scroll to the sect. Again, the matter is much debated.

Now I am not going to discuss the fact that, when they were scrambling around in the caves, when they went up and down the Jordan Valley, the Rift Valley, they found inscriptions in other valleys, not just in the Wadi Qumran. These scroll materials are also sometimes called Dead Sea Scrolls, but we are not going to discuss them here, especially since they come from different time periods.

One other footnote: They are still looking for scrolls. There is no certainty that we have found all the scrolls. With new techniques, by going carefully over the area according to a plan, knowing what we are looking for, there may be new finds. The search still goes on and some fragments are still being found.

Now let me talk briefly about the publication problem. These scholars are brilliant, conscientious men, they have worked hard, but they have not managed to make significant progress on the Cave 4 texts. The worst part of it is that there is a scholarly convention that provides that, until the material is published by the scholar who was assigned to publish it, no one else can see it without that scholar's permission.*

These treasures belong to all of us. These scholars did not find them. It is not as if they are archaeologists who excavated them. Nowhere is this convention written down. You can't read about it. You don't know the limits of it. You don't know how long it lasts. In the November 1990 issue of *Scientific American*, there is a story on this. Frank Cross, one of the great scholars working on these texts, a wonderful man and a member of the original team, is quoted as saying, "Normally

---

* See "The Dead Sea Scroll Monopoly Must Be Broken," *Biblical Archaeology Review*, July/August 1990.

this exclusive right to publish lasts an entire lifetime." This is unbelievable to me.

As a matter of fact, some scholars have asserted this right beyond the grave, as it were. Several scholars have died and have bequeathed their rights. And still you can't see these texts without the permission of their scholarly heirs.

What these unpublished texts contain, we don't know. But let me give you an example of one text. John Strugnell, who is now the chief editor of the scrolls publication team,* announced nearly seven years ago that he had a letter, known as MMT, the only letter that has ever been found in the Qumran caves. He had this text for 25 years and no one knew it. This letter promises to revolutionize Qumran studies. Now you would imagine that when he announced it he would say, "Hey, I have this tremendous letter, maybe I didn't realize it, maybe I did, maybe I should have told you earlier, but in any event, I've got it here, it's 120 lines, let me give you my translation of it, here it is."

That is not how it works.** He announced its existence at some scholarly conventions and as he described it he gave his interpretation of it. But you can't see it! Here it is seven years later and he has continued to talk about it. There is no question as to its importance. People who have seen it, and Strugnell himself, say that you can't exaggerate its importance. It is so important that seven or eight copies of this letter were kept at Qumran and have survived at least in part. It tells us about the origins of this sectarian group, about the history of rabbinic Judaism, about the Pharisees and Sadducees—all by implication.

John Strugnell is a great scholar and he certainly knows Hebrew, but his Hebrew linguistics in this particular area might not be all that he would like, so he has associated a great Israeli scholar by the name of Elisha Qimron in his project and together they have written a commentary on this 120-line text. According to *Scientific American*, the commentary is 600 pages long. Until they finish and publish their commentary, you cannot see this text.† Despite Strugnell's brilliance and knowledge, he is limited in certain areas. He is not an expert in Jewish religious law and this letter contains 20 or so religious laws. So Strugnell has brought in a scholar from Hebrew University by the name of Ya'akov Sussman to work on the Jewish religious law aspects of the text. Strugnell is not an expert in the calendar; a special calendar was used at Qumran,

---

* Strugnell has since been relieved of his position. See "Who Controls the Scrolls?" *Biblical Archaeology Review*, March/April 1991.

** See "The Difference Between Scholarly Mistakes and Scholarly Concealment: The Case of MMT," *Biblical Archaeology Review*, September/October 1990.

† But see "Samizdat Dead Sea Scroll for Sale," *Biblical Archaeology Review*, March/April 1991, page 57.

so he brought in another scholar by the name of Shemaryahu Talmon to work on the calendrical aspects of it. In this way, he controls the entire research on this crucial document.

Then Strugnell goes about showing it to a few other scholars. These scholars can then write articles about the text. One of them, a great scholar by the name of Larry Schiffman, has written an article on this text for *Bible Review*,* which I edit. It is a wonderful article, but unless Strugnell says Okay, Jim Sanders or Jim VanderKam or Kyle McCarter, all of whom you are going to hear from today (and who have a different relationship with John Strugnell than I do), can't see it. The scholarly world as a whole still can't see that text. We are still awaiting its publication. We can't see it until it is published. And that is something that has been available for nearly 40 years.

I'm asked time and again, Why? These guys could be heroes. Why don't they open up. I don't understand it myself. An American philanthropic foundation offered $100,000 to publish photographs of the unpublished texts so that all scholars could have a go at them.** The people who still control the texts have had a 30- to 35-year head start on everyone else. There is a tremendous interest in the scholarly community in these texts. A scholar in Kansas has assembled over 10,000 articles that have been written about the Dead Sea Scrolls. That is the kind of interest you have.

Regardless of what subject you deal with in this period, you have to consult these scrolls because they can affect your research—whether it is early Christianity or rabbinic Judaism, the history of the period, linguistics, Hebrew language, mysticism or dualism or apocalypticism, messianism—you name it. You could be in studies relating to Egypt or Greece in this period and you still must look at the Dead Sea Scrolls to see if they affect, or throw light on, what you are researching. For two generations now, scholars have had to proceed with one hand tied behind their back, fearful that the next thing that is published from the Dead Sea Scrolls will contradict what they say, unable to take account of what is in the remainder of the Dead Sea Scrolls.

In the few minutes that are remaining, I do want to say one more thing on the publication problem. The way that the scholars who control the texts have sought to meet the worldwide criticism is to bring in some other scholars, usually students of theirs. Some of these scholars

---

* See Lawrence H. Schiffman, "The Significance of the Scrolls," *Bible Review*, October 1990; see also James C. VanderKam, "The People of the Dead Sea Scrolls: Essenes or Sadducees?" *Bible Review*, April 1991.

** "Scroll Editors Spurn $100,000 Offer to Publish Book of Photographs," *Biblical Archaeology Review*, July/August 1990; "Israel's Antiquities Authority Sides with Recalcitrant Scholars," *Biblical Archaeology Review*, January/February 1991.

are extremely arrogant. Strugnell has just called Geza Vermes, a full professor at Oxford and one of the world's leading Dead Sea Scroll scholars—Strugnell has called Vermes "incompetent."* Another scholar on the team has said that only they are competent to edit the scrolls.** Strugnell himself has said that nobody at Tel Aviv University is qualified to edit one Dead Sea Scroll.† This is the attitude they take. And yet, at the same time, they will give a text to their own graduate students who supposedly are competent because they have better direction. But one of the fine scholars to whom a subassignment has been made is one of our speakers, Jim VanderKam, and Jim has made a major breakthrough. He has said publicly that anybody can see his unpublished texts. And I think that that is a courageous stand and highly commendable.

Let me spend a few minutes on the Temple Scroll because it illustrates one of the problems. The Temple Scroll describes the future building of the Temple. It has a section describing the limits on the authority of the king of Israel. In many passages that are also found in the canonical Hebrew Bible, where the Hebrew Bible says, "Moses said"— Moses got the word from God; the Temple Scroll says, "I said"—God Himself is speaking in the Temple Scroll. The Temple Scroll also tends to harmonize and combine various sections of the canonical Hebrew Bible. There are some people who say that the Temple Scroll is a sectarian document.†† It is clearly a Bible-like document.§

But now listen to the arguments that it is not a sectarian document. There were 25 copies of Deuteronomy found at Qumran, in fragmentary form, 18 copies of Isaiah, 27 copies of the Psalter. Yet if this Temple Scroll is, as often claimed, a critical, crucial document of this sect, why is it that we have only this one fairly complete copy and fragments of possibly two others? I mentioned the letter known as MMT, which was found in seven or eight copies, and yet not so the Temple Scroll. If it were truly a sectarian document, wouldn't we expect to find at least fragments of more copies? Moreover, in Cave 4 not a single copy of the Temple Scroll was found. If it was a sectarian document, why wouldn't it be there? And there are no quotes from the Temple Scroll in other sectarian documents; this is not the case with

---

* "Strugnell Calls Leading Scroll Scholar Incompetent," *Biblical Archaeology Review*, January/February 1991.

** "The Dead Sea Scroll Monopoly Must Be Broken," *Biblical Archaeology Review*, July/August 1990.

† "No One at Tel Aviv University Qualified to Edit Dead Sea Scrolls," *Biblical Archaeology Review*, January/February 1990.

†† Yigael Yadin, "The Temple Scroll—The Longest and Most Recently Discovered Dead Sea Scroll," *Biblical Archaeology Review*, September/October 1984.

§ Hartmut Stegemann, "Is the Temple Scroll a Sixth Book of the Torah—Lost for 2,500 Years?" *Biblical Archaeology Review*, November/December 1987.

other sectarian documents. This, too, indicates that the Temple Scroll is not a sectarian document. The sect supposedly represented in this supposedly sectarian document was opposed to the Jerusalem Temple. The priests of the Jerusalem Temple were their enemies. But there is nothing in the Temple Scroll which reflects any animosity to the Temple. So why should we think it is a sectarian document?

This is the kind of analysis that we are going through to find out what these texts mean. Were they sectarian or were they not? If so, what sect? And where did the library come from? Some people, as I said earlier, say that these documents were produced at Qumran. Is it really likely that this little desert community produced, or even owned, a library of 800 scrolls? I think not.

The time period we are talking about is from about 250 B.C.E. to about 68 C.E. We know the end of it pretty clearly because the settlement was destroyed in about 68 C.E., during the Roman suppression of the First Jewish Revolt. And Jerusalem was destroyed in 70 C.E. The Temple was burned by the Romans.

I think that this library was a Jerusalem library. We know that on many occasions the Judean wilderness was a place of refuge. People ran away there. We know from the Bible that David ran there to escape, and Saul pursued him. Other documents have been found elsewhere in the wilderness. We know that documents were taken there and hidden time and again. So I think that the most likely answer is that these documents were in a Jerusalem library. They were taken to Qumran for safekeeping. Then the settlement itself was destroyed.

But that still does not tell us the nature of the library. One scholar feels that these documents represent mainstream Judaism of the time, a general picture of Judaism. Most scholars think that the sectarian documents belong to a sect that was opposed to the Temple, that had its own calendar and its own holidays.

Then why did they have these other documents there in this library? Various answers have been suggested.

There is no question, however, that this library gives us a new view, a direct view of the people that were there at the time, a new view of Judaism of the time, of the Judaism that was the forerunner of both rabbinic Judaism and early Christianity. We used to say that Christianity was a daughter religion of Judaism. Now there is a different way of expressing that idea and perhaps a more accurate one.

The picture we get from the Qumran documents is of a much more varied Judaism before the Roman destruction than we had ever imagined. It is almost inaccurate to talk about Judaism. Many scholars talk about Judaisms. We find not only a dedication to law but to messianism, apocalypticism, the end of days, mysticism, a whole range of beliefs, dualism. Many of these ideas we thought Christianity took from later Hellenistic sources, outside Palestine. Now we know that there were sources right in Palestine from which they could have been absorbed into Christianity. The picture that is emerging is that after the destruction of 70 C.E. by the Romans, both rabbinic Judaism and messianic Christianity emerged with their roots in different pre-70 strains of Judaism. In that sense, they are sister religions, both going back to Second Temple Jewish sources of which the Qumran documents are the greatest contemporaneous exemplars that we have. We are just now beginning to be able to trace that development. It is a very exciting time for the next generation of scholars. I only hope that they will have all the materials at their disposal as soon as possible. Thank you.

Questions & Answers

How were the publication assignments made?

I think that there are two aspects to the question. First, how did the scrolls get to the Rockefeller Museum? The purchase money to get the scrolls from the Bedouin was put up by various national schools who thought that they would eventually have the right to exhibit a show of the scrolls at their own particular school. But the scrolls were all taken to the Rockefeller first to be studied. Then once they were there, this team of scholars simply divvied them up on an arbitrary basis. I think *Time* magazine made a reference to J. T. Milik, who was then a Polish priest, as the fastest draw with a fragment. He has since left the priesthood. He got the biggest hunk of the texts and he still has the most cherished documents. As a matter of fact, it was public pressure that finally led to his giving up some of his documents, and he has given up some to Jim VanderKam who we are going to hear from. The original team members apparently sat in a room and said who wants this one? And Milik said, "I'll take that one." That is how it was done.

What about Solomon Zeitlin, who claimed the scrolls were medieval forgeries?

His ideas have been completely demolished. There is no one of standing in the scholarly community who subscribes to that. He based his arguments on some linguistic forms which he said did not appear until medieval times. But the fact that they were there in the scrolls demonstrates that they were indeed used earlier.

The scrolls are dated by a variety of techniques. Most accurately today they are dated paleographically. We have enough different styles of writing, the shape of the letters, the stance of the letters, so that within 50 or 75 years—there are some arguments as to just how close you can do it, but within 50 to 75 years—you can date writing just by looking at the letters. Experts can do this. The three scholars who are going to talk to you today are people who can do it.

You also have the evidence from the nearby settlement: the shape of the jars that they were found in, carbon-14 tests on the linen that they were wrapped in. We are doing carbon-14 tests now on the scrolls themselves to try to get an even more accurate date, but there is some unanimity. The documents date no later than about 68 C.E. and they go back to about 250 B.C.E., so it is very early. Don't forget you have to distinguish between the date of the copy and the date the text was composed, just as we do with the Bible. Your Bible may have been printed in 1987, but the text was written thousands of years ago. In the same way, you may have a text from Qumran that was written in 100 B.C.E., but was actually composed 200 years earlier.

What does it mean to say that any particular document is sectarian?

You may get different answers from the scholars who will appear later. There is a consensus among scholars that there seems to be a core of documents which represent a body of thinking that is narrower and different from the Judaism we know about from later sources and from other texts. Because of their calendar and because of the outlook, because of the style, you can isolate within the larger library a group of documents that seems to have governed one sect of Jews. The borders of that are very difficult. I gave you an example—the Temple Scroll—as to which there is a difference of opinion.

As a matter of fact, one very prominent scholar I have already mentioned, Larry Schiffman, says that the Qumran sect traces back to the Sadducees, who are mentioned in the New Testament and in Josephus as a major sect of Jews at the time. Larry says that either we have to redefine what we mean by Essene or conclude that the sect is really a Saducean sect. Those are some of the kinds of problems that you get in defining what the sectarian documents are. Larry bases his conclusions largely on the unpublished text I have referred to, MMT, and it is difficult for other scholars to judge his ideas because they do not have access to MMT.

Introduction

*I*n the last year or so, J. T. Milik in Paris decided to divest himself of some his treasures, including his texts of the Book of Jubilees. He chose to assign those texts to one of the world's leading authorities on the Book of Jubilees. Our next speaker, who, as I have said in my own talk, has agreed to make his texts available to anyone who wishes to see them, holds a Ph.D. from Harvard University. He is presently a professor of religion at North Carolina State University, where he has taught since 1976. [He is now a professor at the University of Notre Dame.] He has also taught at the University of St. Andrews (Scotland) and the University of California in San Diego. His publications are numerous—scholarly books and monographs as well as articles. He is probably the world's greatest authority on the Book of Jubilees and also a leading scholar on the First Book of Enoch. He is going to talk to us today on the implications of the Qumran texts for the history of Judaism and Christianity. Jim VanderKam. —H.S.

JAMES C. VANDERKAM

Implications for the History of Judaism and Christianity

S HERSHEL MENTIONED, MY assignment is to talk about the scrolls and their implications for the history of Judaism and Christianity. Perhaps half or two-thirds of the way through, I will show some pictures of the Dead Sea Scroll text that I am dealing with so you may see what the scrolls look like, and also to prove that I meant it when I said that I would show them to anyone who wants to see them.

I propose to do three things in the time allotted to me. I want to survey what the scrolls have already done for us—how they have increased our knowledge in three areas: our knowledge of Jewish groups in the late Second Temple period—that is, the last centuries before the Common Era and the first century of the Common Era; our knowledge of Jewish literature from that time; and also our understanding of the Semitic background of the New Testament.

First, the Jewish groups of this period. I doubt that anyone who is historically knowledgeable would object to my saying that the last two centuries Before the Common Era and the first century of the Common Era were of extraordinary significance for Judaism and Christianity, and thus for Western culture in general. But despite the amazing importance of those centuries, our source material for them has been rather scanty, surprisingly so. We learn from some of those sources that the two leading parties, or groups, among the Jews at that time were the Sadducees and the Pharisees. But, perhaps with one or two exceptions, no Sadducean or Pharisaic document has survived. We learn about them only through the reports of others—reports that are at times hostile (usually that is true of the New Testament), sometimes written considerably later (the Mishnah and the Talmuds) and always biased (the first-century Jewish historian Josephus is a good example).

W hile several ancient writers tell us about the Pharisees and the Sadducees, fewer mention the Essenes, the third of the major groups according to Josephus. Though Essenes are mentioned less frequently than the other two parties, they may today have an advantage over their more famous rivals. According to most scholars, as you have already heard, the people of Qumran, the ones who wrote and copied the scrolls, were Essenes. They are the only Jewish group from that time to bequeath to us a library (or, at least, a library was hidden in the Qumran settlement area). We should be in a position to learn more about the views of the Essenes from their own pens than we know about the other groups. We don't learn about the Essenes through the distortions of others; we learn about them from their own biases. So the little-known Essenes may now have emerged into a brighter public light than any of their fellows.

I said that most people have accepted the view that the community of the scrolls were Essenes. Actually, in the 40 years or so of the history of research into the scrolls, people have made all sorts of claims. Some have said the people of the scroll community were Pharisees, some have said they were Sadducees, most have identified them as Essenes, some have even claimed they were Christians, although of an odd type—in a whole library there is no mention of Jesus.

You could object that putting a label on the group is not terribly important. Whatever name we give to the group, it does not change what the scrolls say. A rose by any other name. . . . But I do want to deal with this issue of the party affiliation of this group because it is very much under discussion today, as Hershel has indicated, with some claiming that the group was Sadducean (in origin at least), rather than Essene. So I want to look into that, to examine the evidence that scholars have used to identify the group as Essene; I want to look at the recent arguments for saying the group was of Sadducean origin; and then perhaps say something about the circumstances that may have led to the origin of this particular group.

Very early in the history of scholarship on the scrolls, the proposal was made that this group was Essene. The evidence was of two kinds: The first came from the report of Pliny the Elder, the Roman scholar who had apparently visited this area and described the Essenes; the second was the content of the scrolls themselves as compared with the descriptions that we have of the ancient Essenes, particularly from Josephus, the first-century Jewish historian. Pliny the Elder is the only ancient writer who meets two conditions: A book of his is preserved and he mentions what I think must be the Qumran group. In his book *Natural History* he wrote:

> On the west side of the Dead Sea, but out of range of the noxious exhalations of the coast, is the solitary tribe of the Essenes, which is remarkable beyond all the other tribes in the whole world, as it has no women and has renounced all sexual desire, has no money, and has only palm trees for company. Day by day the throng of refugees is recruited to an equal number by numerous accessions of persons tired of life and driven thither by the waves of fortune to adopt their manners. Thus through thousands of ages (incredible to relate), a race in which no one is born lives on forever; so prolific for their advantage is other men's weariness of life! Lying below them [that is, these Essenes] was formerly the town of Engedi.*

Pliny then goes on to describe Ein Gedi (as it is now known) and what happened to it. So he is describing a spot south of Jericho on the northwest side of the Dead Sea; and he said he met Essenes out there. Qumran is the only archaeological site in the area that meets the qualifications of having buildings that might have accommodated a community and of being north of Ein Gedi. Pliny said he found Essenes there, and he took the trouble to become informed about their way of life—or perhaps the source that he is quoting did.

There are objections that scholars have raised against the conclusion that Pliny, or his source, had visited the Qumran community; also, there are some problems in the text that we need not go into here.** But I can assure you that all of the problems can be fairly easily handled, and when all is said and done, we have a pleasant surprise: An ancient Roman author, who would have no reason to fabricate the report, found a community of Essenes living alone on the northwest shore of the Dead Sea where Qumran lies. Pliny's reports about this group show the same things we find in their own texts and elsewhere about the ancient Essenes. That is one argument.

The second argument for identifying this group as Essenes comes from the texts themselves—that is, the sectarian texts (and we have already heard why that is a somewhat difficult concept)—as compared

---

* Pliny, *Natural History* 2, transl. H. Rackham, Loeb Classical Library (London: Heinemann/ Cambridge, MA: Harvard Univ. Press, 1969), 5.15, 73.

** See now James VanderKam, "The People of the Dead Sea Scrolls: Essenes or Sadducees?" *Bible Review*, April 1991.

with what Josephus said about the Essenes. What the texts from Qumran say coincides much more closely with Essene thought and action as described in our sources than with their statements about the Pharisees and Sadducees.

The most important text in these comparisons has been one of those from the first cave, the Manual of Discipline, as it is called—a scroll that has been around for a long time. Photographs of it were already available in 1951 when Millar Burrows published them.* They were made available by the American Schools of Oriental Research (ASOR), a group that has been very prominent in the publication of the scrolls. The Manual of Discipline describes among other topics some of the fundamental beliefs of the group, the initiation processes and ceremonies for new members and the rules that governed their daily life and gatherings.

One point on which the descriptions of the Essenes and the Manual of Discipline show striking agreement is the doctrine of Fate, or predestination. Josephus wrote that the three Jewish parties held differing views on this score. He says,

> As for the Pharisees, they say that certain things are the work of Fate but not all; as to other events, it depends upon ourselves whether they shall take place or not. The sect of the Essenes, however, declares that Fate is mistress of all things, and that nothing befalls men unless it be in accordance with her decree. But the Sadducees do away with Fate, holding that there is no such thing and that human actions are not achieved in accordance with her decree, but that all things lie within our own power so that we ourselves are responsible for our well-being, while we suffer misfortune through our own thoughtlessness.**

The third and fourth columns of the Manual of Discipline articulate a strongly predestinarian theology of world history and human endeavor. For example,

> From the God of Knowledge comes all that is and shall be. Before ever they existed He established their whole design, and when, as ordained for them, they came into being, it is in accord with His glorious design that they accomplish their task without change.

There are plenty of other texts among the scrolls that make the same point. I think it is important to remember that such sentiments put the Qumran group furthest from the Sadducean position, some-

* Millar Burrows, *The Dead Sea Scrolls of St. Mark's Monastery*, vol. II, fasc. 2 (New Haven, CT: American Schools of Oriental Research, 1951).

** Josephus, *Jewish Antiquities*, transl. Ralph Marcus, Loeb Classical Library (London: Heinemann/Cambridge, MA: Harvard Univ. Press, 1966), 13.5, 9, 171-173.

what nearer the Pharisaic and dead center on that of the Essenes.

From theological points of this sort to other more mundane topics, the series of resemblances continues. For example, Josephus mentions the Essenes' common ownership of property. He says,

> Riches they despise, and their community of goods is truly admirable; you will not find one among them distinguished by greater opulence than another. They have a law that new members on admission to the sect shall confiscate their property to the order, with the result that you will nowhere see either abject poverty or inordinate wealth; the individual's possessions join the common stock and all, like brothers, enjoy a single patrimony.*

The Manual of Discipline also indicates that when a person entered the community, after passing through a certain period of initiation, he handed over his property to the group. It was then recorded, but it was not used by the group for another year. Only when the novice had passed through the final stage was his property, as the text says, "merged" with that of the community.

Now there are perhaps some small differences between what Josephus and the Manual of Discipline say about how one became an Essene, but scholars have been impressed by the fact that Josephus and the scrolls, in this case the Manual of Discipline, agree on something as trivial as spitting in a group assembly. They both deal with this subject and both say it was prohibited by the Essenes. I don't know if that distinguished them from other groups, but both sources do mention it. Josephus says: "They are careful not to spit into the midst of the company or to the right." The Manual of Discipline says: "Whoever has spat in an Assembly of the Congregation shall do penance for thirty days."

More examples could be added but let me conclude this comparison by noting what Todd Beall wrote in a recent dissertation; in comparing Josephus' descriptions of the Essenes and the scrolls themselves, he found 27 parallels between Josephus and the scrolls, 21 probable parallels, 10 cases in which Josephus makes claims about the Essenes that have no known parallel in the scrolls and 6 discrepancies between them.** In two of the six discrepancies, he goes on to say, the scrolls themselves do not agree with one another, and it is particularly the Manual of Discipline and the Damascus Document—two of the more important communal texts—that disagree. The Damascus Document, for example, seems to presuppose that individuals have private property. The Damascus Document, however, may refer to a different kind

---

* Josephus, *The Jewish War*, transl. H. St.J. Thackeray, Loeb Classical Library (London: Heinemann/Cambridge, MA: Harvard Univ. Press, 1976), 2.8, 3, 122.

** Todd Beall, *Josephus' Description of the Essenes Illustrated by the Dead Sea Scrolls*, Society for New Testament Studies Monograph 58 (Cambridge, UK: Cambridge Univ. Press, 1988).

of Essene than the type living at Qumran. Nevertheless the parallels are very, very close between Josephus' description of the Essenes and what the documents themselves say. This, I think, is a powerful argument in favor of the identification.

There are a couple of things which should be said about this, though. As we have noted before, you have to establish which texts are sectarian before you do such a comparison. I think this can be done by starting out with an undoubted example—like the Manual of Discipline—and then extrapolating from it to other texts that do, in fact, seem to be sectarian—although there is going to be some debate on the issue. Also, we can only compare two texts on points that are covered by both authors. Perhaps if we had more information, other configurations would appear.

It is mildly disturbing to me that there are some very noticeable traits in the scrolls that neither Josephus nor any other ancient cataloguer of Essene beliefs noted. I have in mind in particular the 364-day solar calendar which this group followed and which is mentioned in several texts from Qumran. There is also their belief that two Messiahs would be part of the end of days. Josephus does not mention either of these matters but both of them do occur in important texts from Qumran.

It is often said that Josephus does not tell us about such things because he didn't think his Greco-Roman audience would be interested. In addition, he does not report that sort of material for any of the other groups he discusses. But one wonders whether his audience would have been more interested in the avoidance of spitting during communal gatherings than subjects like this—and Josephus chose to report on that one. Where differences exist between Josephus and the Qumran texts, it may be that Josephus merely reflects later versions of Essene beliefs than we get in some of these texts. He was writing in the late first century C.E., whereas some of our communal texts come from nearly 200 years before that. It is hardly credible that all Essenes agreed on everything and that their views remained static over some 200 years.

But today I think most would agree with Frank Cross's assessment—at least on my reading of what people are saying. He accepts the Essene identification and says:

> The scholar who would "exercise caution" in identifying the sect of Qumran with the Essenes places himself in an astonishing position; he must suggest seriously that two major parties each formed communistic religious communities in the same district of the desert of the Dead Sea and lived together in effect for two centuries, holding similar bizarre views, performing similar or rather identical lustrations, ritual meals, and ceremonies. Further, the scholar must suppose that one community, carefully described by classical authors, disappeared without leaving

building remains or even potsherds behind; while the other community, systematically ignored by the classical sources, left extensive ruins and even a great library.*

So, Cross says: "I prefer to be reckless and flatly identify the men of Qumran with their perennial houseguests, the Essenes." I agree.

This is the sort of information that has led to the traditional identification of these people as Essenes. The Cross lecture from which I quoted was given in 1966, and a lot has changed since then. The Temple Scroll, about which you've heard, has been published. The document called 4QMMT is available in numerous photocopies, and a lot of us have seen it. It, too, is causing something of a sensation. The editors of MMT claim that it may be a letter from the leader of the Qumran group, the Teacher of Righteousness, writing on behalf of his group to their opponents in Jerusalem and distinguishing their legal views. In this text, some 20 or 22 legal positions are raised. Thus, one can learn something definite from the text about the legal posturing of one group over against the other.

As Hershel mentioned a short while ago, Lawrence Schiffman of New York University has been arguing, especially on the basis of this unpublished letter, that the people of Qumran have significant overlaps with what the Mishnah (written in about 200 C.E.) says the Sadducees believed.** He thinks this makes it necessary for us to re-examine the whole issue of the origins of the Qumran group and whether they really were Essenes and not Sadducees originally. He refers in particular to a section of the Mishnah in which several disputes between the Pharisees and the Sadducees are mentioned. For example, it starts out by saying:

> The Sadducees say, We cry out against you, O ye Pharisees, for ye say, "The Holy Scriptures render the hands unclean," [and] "The writings of Hamiram [which may be a textual error for the name Homer or secular writings] do not render the hands unclean." . . . And, the Sadducees say, We cry out against you, O ye Pharisees, for ye declare clean an unbroken stream of liquid (*Yadayim* 4, 6-7).

Apparently the Sadducees and the Pharisees disagreed on whether a stream of liquid poured from a clean vessel into an unclean one conveyed the uncleanness of the receptacle back into the original one, with the Sadducees claiming that it did and the Pharisees denying it. There are a variety of disputes like this—four or five in all. From comparing what these disputes have to say with what 4QMMT has to say,

---

* Frank Moore Cross, "The Early History of the Qumran Community," in *New Directions in Biblical Archaeology*, ed. David Noel Freedman and Jonas C. Greenfield (Garden City, NY: Doubleday, 1971), p. 77.

** Lawrence H. Schiffman, "The Significance of the Scrolls," *Bible Review*, October 1990.

Schiffman says that in every place where they talk about the same topic, these people from Qumran seem to have the same view as the Sadducees are said to have had in this particular Mishnah.

I will readily agree that Schiffman is much better at reading the Mishnah and the new legal text than I am. But from my look at these, it is very difficult for me to find any necessary connection between what is attributed to the Sadducees in the first dispute and what is said in 4QMMT. In one case—the one about the liquid stream that I was just mentioning—the position argued in the 4QMMT is the position attributed to the Sadducees in the Mishnah. About the others, the case is less clear. Now there is this overlap in one case and there are probably others. Let's be generous. What can we say about the agreement between what this Qumran text says is the legal view of this community and what was attributed to the Sadducees? We cannot make much of it. Even if the Sadducees and this group from Qumran agreed on every one of these legal points, I still think that not much could be done with it or concluded from it because I presume that Essenes and Sadducees did agree on a lot of points.

The reason is that they have similar origins in the priestly class among the ancient Jewish population. It is very clear that the people of Qumran considered their leaders to be priests, the sons of Zadok as they say. The Sadducees derived their name, it seems, from the same biblical priest, Zadok. So we do have some overlaps between this Essene group and what was attributed to the Sadducees. But I hardly think that this means that we therefore have to say that we had better give up the Essene thesis because Essenes and Sadducees did not disagree about everything. Also, I doubt that any of these cases are cases of fundamental importance.

What I find particularly objectionable about Schiffman's position is that he ignores all of the evidence that has gone into the traditional identification of the people of the scrolls as Essenes. Some views expressed in the scrolls—even in a very early one such as the Manual of Discipline—are diametrically opposed to those of the Sadducees. How, if Schiffman is correct, did these traditionalists change their minds so swiftly and so completely?

I think what the literature (about the parties) is showing us is an actual Essene group. And I don't even say Essenoid—they look Essene to me. It also indicates that this group was opposed to the Pharisees.

The Qumran texts have made an enormous contribution to the literature of the Second Temple period. Let me distinguish some areas. In connection with the biblical text, of course, the contribution has been overwhelming and some of this has already been discussed. We have in the Qumran texts our most ancient copies of biblical books. It has been said this morning that all the books of the Hebrew Bible except

Esther are attested by at least one fragment from the caves.

I want to urge some caution in that kind of a statement. It's true as it stands, but there are a couple of terms that need some clarification—terms that may not seem to need definition. One is the word "book." That should be pretty clear, you'd think. Who doesn't know what a book is? But, some books that are distinguished in our Bibles, like Ezra and Nehemiah, were regarded as one book in early Jewish tradition. When people say that there is only one book of the Old Testament that is not attested at Qumran (Esther), it is assumed that at that time, Ezra and Nehemiah were already considered one book. It turns out that we have a few fragments of Ezra but nothing of Nehemiah. So if you were especially anxious to see fragments of Nehemiah, do not hold your breath.

This is true in the case of the minor prophets, too—the Book of the Twelve Prophets—not the most familiar books in the Hebrew Bible. Some of those small prophetic books have not shown up either, but if we assume that all 12 were considered one book, as they were at one time, then the statement is true—the Book of the Twelve Prophets is attested, but not all of its individual parts.

Also, I think you should be aware that the word "Bible" is not entirely clear. It is not clear that the people who lived at Qumran had exactly the same limits on what constituted the Bible as any group does today. Let me show you some of the evidence that suggests this. There are a couple of texts that were found among the Dead Sea Scrolls that scholars today classify as pseudepigrapha. I have in mind here especially First Enoch and the Book of Jubilees. Both of these pseudepigraphic books—the one attributed to Enoch, the sixth from Adam [Genesis 5:3-18], who lived before the Flood; the other, Jubilees, attributed to Moses—advertise themselves as divine revelations mediated through angels to these great heroes of the Bible.

Now nobody believes that those biblical heroes wrote those books—they came into existence much later. But copies of them were found among the scrolls, and I think the number of copies found of each one is significant. First Enoch is represented in the caves of Qumran by 11 copies. Seven of them have excerpts from the smaller booklets—four of them parts of the very long astronomical Book of Luminaries of First Enoch.*

If J. T. Milik, the editor of this text, is correct, First Enoch also included the Book of Giants, which is found in six more copies, one of

---

* First Enoch in its present form is divided into five sections: Book of Watchers, Book of Similitudes (or Parables), Book of Luminaries (containing astronomical data), Dream Visions and Epistle of Enoch (or Book of Admonitions). Second and Third Enoch are believed to have been written later. In any event no copies of them have been found at Qumran.

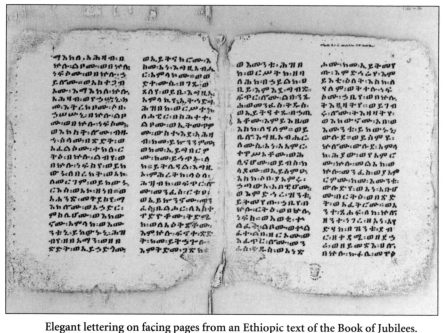

Elegant lettering on facing pages from an Ethiopic text of the Book of Jubilees. *Written in Hebrew, perhaps around 150 B.C.E., Jubilees was translated into Greek and then into Ethiopic, a Semitic language similar to Hebrew. The text of Jubilees survives in its entirety only in Ethiopic. The Ethiopic Christian Church—isolated from the rest of the church for centuries—considers Jubilees part of the Old Testament. Some scholars speculate that the Ethiopic canon may reflect an earlier period of the Christian church when the biblical canon was more inclusive. Twenty-seven complete manuscripts of Jubilees exist; this one, from the British Library, is probably the best. It helps modern scholars piece together Hebrew fragments of Jubilees found at Qumran.* Courtesy of James C. VanderKam

which may overlap with the 11 mentioned above. A similar situation prevails for the Book of Jubilees—fragments of which I am currently editing.

Just to give you some relief from listening to me, let's look at some pictures of the Book of Jubilees—the fragments that we have of it.

Those of you who know Hebrew should be aware that the script in this picture is not Hebrew; these pages were not found at Qumran. The Book of Jubilees was written in Hebrew, maybe around 150 B.C.E. That text was lost. It was translated into Greek, but that text has been lost. From Greek it was translated into Ethiopic, and that text has been preserved in its entirety because the Ethiopic Christian Church considered it part of the Old Testament. So there are quite a few copies of this book available in Ethiopic; in fact, 27 of them. I know every one and I am very tired of reading them. This is what they look like. This is from the copy of Jubilees that the British Library has—probably the best copy. This is one part of a very long book; it is as long as the Book of Genesis. But I think the Ethiopic script has to qualify as one of the most beautiful there is when a professional scribe does it. Ethiopic is a Semitic language, so if you know Hebrew it is not too big a jump into this. You just have to learn 270 new symbols or so. The next picture [page 30] shows fragments of the Book of Jubilees from Qumran—all from Cave 4. This comes from the first copy, copy A, and it is the oldest one that we have. I want to pay tribute to J. T. Milik whom I consider an awesome scholar, even though his pace of production has not been as fast as we would like, and probably not as fast as he would like either. He is responsible for identifying these copies, for lining them up as they are. He read the texts, and he has done a lot of work on them. One of the interesting things about this particular manuscript for me is that you can still see the thread that holds the two sheets together.

If you are really into Hebrew scripts you can see that the script on one side of the fragment differs from the script on the other side. Apparently the outside sheet of this manuscript became worn and had to be replaced. So the old sheet was taken off and someone copied the text from it onto a newer piece of parchment. It was then sewn onto the manuscript, and so we have the two different scribal hands in one manuscript. The fact they are still sewn together shows that they did indeed belong to one manuscript. If we had found them in isolation, it would have been assumed that they belonged to two.

Milik identified another set of fragments as a text of Jubilees. I have my doubts about this one. I have not completed my work on it, but I doubt that it is Jubilees. One piece I am working on right now seems like a very nice, big fragment. You would think that something like this would not take any time to do. It is a nice text, in that it agrees with the Ethiopic text very closely. The trouble is that at the end of one of the lines where I cannot see anything, Milik has indicated that he very clearly saw three or four letters; he does not even indicate that there is any question about them. I absolutely cannot see them.

Those are just some of the fragments that I have. Milik has given me all of the Jubilees fragments and some related texts as well. I mention these texts to you because on Milik's count there are 15 manuscripts of Jubilees found at Qumran. On my count there are 14. That is an impressive number. If we compare these statistics to the numbers available for various biblical books, the comparison is revealing. The Book of Psalms is represented by the most copies. The latest numbers I have seen are that 30 copies of Psalms have been identified, followed by Deuteronomy with 25 and Isaiah with 19. Genesis and Exodus are present in 15 copies. No other biblical book breaks into double digits,

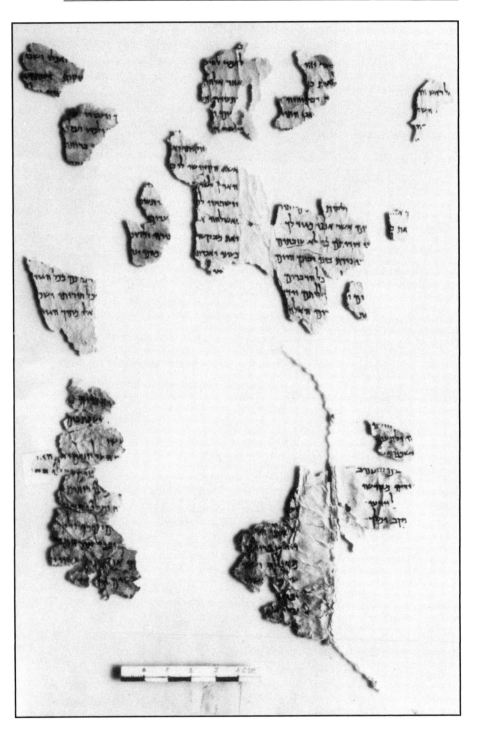

Never before published text from Jubilees. *These Hebrew fragments from the Book of Jubilees, found in Cave 4, are the oldest examples from that book found at Qumran, where 14 manuscripts of Jubilees were discovered. Notice that the Hebrew script to the right of the stitching differs from the script on the left. Apparently the outside page of this manuscript became worn and had to be replaced. The worn sheet was removed and a different scribe copied the text onto a newer piece of cured animal skin. At the lower right, the thread used to sew the new page to the old one provided scholars with the evidence that enabled them to conclude that texts from different scribes were part of the same scroll. Without that thread scholars would have assumed that the fragments belonged to two different scrolls. The Biblical Archaeology Society is grateful to Professor VanderKam for making available this previously unpublished photograph.*
Courtesy of James C. VanderKam

but both First Enoch and Jubilees do. This means that there were more copies of those books at Qumran than of almost any other book that we now have in our Bible.

It does not necessarily follow that just because a book is present in a large number of copies that therefore it must have been considered biblical or authoritative, but I suspect that there is a correlation. Why would we have so many copies if they were not considered important? And when we add that both of these books, First Enoch and Jubilees, claim to be divine revelations, something that the Manual of Discipline, for example, does not do, the case for seeing the two books as highly authoritative is strengthened.

Also, both books had an important influence on other Qumran texts. The Book of Enoch provides the calendar—the 364-day calendar—that was followed at Qumran. It talks about the angels of Heaven who descended to earth and mated with the daughters of men before the Flood, a very important story in some Qumran literature and other texts. These are just a few of the influences of First Enoch on other texts at Qumran. Jubilees also had an influence; it is cited as an authority in one of the other Qumran texts—the Damascus Document refers the reader to the Book of Jubilees to find the exact determinations of times in which Israel goes astray. There seems to be another reference or two to Jubilees in other Qumran texts.

So both of these books, First Enoch and Jubilees, are represented in many copies; they claim to be divine revelations; and they influenced other texts among the Dead Sea Scrolls. I think that this suggests that if we could get one of the ancient Essenes before us and ask, what is your Bible—in case he knew what that word meant—he might list books like First Enoch and Jubilees as belonging to that authoritative body of literature to which he would refer and to which he would refer others. It suggests to me, at least, that at the time of this group, the bounds of the canon, to use a later word, were not fixed as they were at a later time. So the question of what exactly was included in the Bible at Qumran remains open.

Another kind of literature that I think is very important at Qumran and that has been mentioned is the commentaries. Many commentaries on biblical books have been found, almost always in one copy. They open our eyes to the serious thought that people gave to the biblical text at Qumran and to the method of interpretation used, the so-called *pesher** method. Among these commentaries, the best known is the commentary on the Book of Habakkuk; a couple of commentaries have been found on the Book of Micah, two on Zephaniah (of all books), four on various Psalms, six on Isaiah, two on Hosea and one on Nahum. Sometimes the comments are on a whole book, sometimes only on part of it and sometimes on selections of passages from various books.

We know that this group spent a lot of time studying Scriptures. These commentaries are evidence of that fact. Some of these commentaries give us the little bits of information that we do have about the history of this group because biblical texts are interpreted as if the ancient biblical prophet was referring to this group of Essenes, to their leader, the Teacher of Righteousness, and to the vicissitudes through which the group went.

Several books of the Apocrypha have been found in fragmentary form at Qumran. The Book of Tobit is present in several copies in two languages, one in Hebrew, the others in Aramaic. Excerpts from the Wisdom of Joshua ben Sira [or Ecclesiasticus] have been found; there is one fragment from Cave 2 that has a few verses from the sixth chapter of the book; in the Psalm Scroll that Professor Sanders has edited, there is a poem that in our text shows up in the Book of Ben Sira, chapter 51. There are some copies of the Testament of the Twelve Patriarchs, a whole book of testaments, or death bed statements, from Jacob's 12 sons. What seem to be the sources (or some of the sources) of the Testament of Levi and the Testament of Naphtali have been found among the Dead Sea Scrolls.

All of these copies of apocryphal and pseudepigraphic books indicate the antiquity of these works, something about the languages in which they were written and something about the sort of community in which such books were copied.

Of course, much of the Qumran library consists of books that were sectarian, or seem to have been—various kinds of rules for the community. In addition many poetic compositions, and their number

---

* Authors of these commentaries believed that the Old Testament books were filled with mysteries that were fulfilled in the history of this community, but the meaning of the mysteries was hidden until revealed by God to the Teacher of Righteousness and his followers.

is only now becoming evident, were perhaps used in the liturgy of the group. Often these are the kinds of texts that you cannot date or in which you cannot find specific sectarian emphases.

A translation into Aramaic (a Targum) of the Book of Leviticus has been found and a good-sized one on the Book of Job. And then there are so many fragmentary texts, texts so small that no one can identify them—maybe they came from something important. There are legal texts that demonstrate a very important point: namely, this group put a great premium on obeying God and obeying God precisely according to the law revealed to Moses—the law found in the Bible and interpreted carefully by this group.

Let me use just a few minutes now in conclusion to talk about the scrolls and what they tell us about the New Testament. As you might imagine, when the scrolls were first found and something of their date became known, all sorts of wild speculation took place on how this community might be related to the New Testament. We even got Jesus out to Qumran. Very few people talk that way anymore, and the ones who do do not carry much weight. If this group at Qumran was Essene, it raises some interesting questions, because in some ways this group shared ideas that the early Christians had. Yet, as we will see, the name Essene is never mentioned in the New Testament. You can look all through the New Testament and you will not find that word. You find Pharisees and Sadducees but not Essenes, at least not under that name.

Scholars were quick to notice that there were traces of Essene practices among the early Christians. One prominent example, of course, was the community of goods that we have talked about already and that the Book of Acts says the early Christians followed. Acts 4:32 says that "the company of those who believed were of one heart and soul, and no one said that any of the things which he possessed was his own, but they had everything in common." Acts goes on to talk about how someone tried to cheat about this, and it cost him his life and that of his wife. A second practice which called attention to itself was the meal which the Essenes were to enjoy in the company of the messiahs—the two messiahs—a meal at which bread and wine were mentioned. You can imagine what that suggested to people; the Eucharist of the New Testament.

Whether the parallels went beyond the simple fact that bread and wine were consumed in the presence of a messiah is debatable. There does not seem to be any indication that the meal of the Essenes was a Passover meal or one at which the bread and the wine were charged with a sacramental kind of significance.

While almost everyone has recognized that Jesus really could not be brought into direct connection with the Qumran Essenes, John the Baptist seemed like a more promising candidate. This strange character was said to have lived in the wilderness where he "wore a garment of camel's hair, and a leather girdle around his waist; and his food was locusts and wild honey. Then went out to him Jerusalem and all Judea and all the region about the Jordan, and they were baptized by him in the river Jordan . . . confessing their sins" (Matthew 3:4-6). Now the location of John's ministry was suggestively close to Qumran. Baptism is mentioned in the scrolls and the confession of sins is reminiscent of the confessions made when the novices entered the Qumran community. Moreover, like the sectaries of Qumran, John operated under the conviction that the end was at hand. All of this adds up to something less than an identification of John as an Essene from Qumran (although people have made that identification and still do today), but it is at least suggestive. It should also not be forgotten that the functions of the Qumran community and of John himself are both explained through use of Isaiah 40:3: The Qumran community and John were both in the wilderness preparing the way of the Lord.

But on a more substantial note, readers of the scrolls and the New Testament were impressed by the unmistakable parallels between the language of light and darkness in the scrolls, especially in the Johannine literature. The sons of light from Qumran who were ruled by the angel of light were in conflict with the sons of darkness who walked in the ways of darkness and were quite appropriately ruled by the angel of darkness. In the Gospel of John, Jesus is presented as the light of the world who came into the darkness which could not overcome him. He urged his followers just before his death: "The light is with you for a little longer. Walk while you have the light, lest the darkness overtake you; he who walks in the darkness does not know where he goes. While you have the light, believe in the light, that you may become sons of light" (John 12:35-36). The designation Jesus uses for his followers in this verse is the one the Qumran people apply to themselves. The language is the same in the two sources as is the content of the words. Light and darkness are metaphors for an ethical dualism of two ways that differ as day does from night.

In the early 1950s, a French scholar, Annie Jaubert, attracted a lot of interest when she proposed that the 364-day calendar of the Essenes provided a solution for an old problem in Gospel research.* The problem was that the Synoptic Gospels on the one hand and John on the other had differing chronologies for the very last days before Jesus' death—a time for which one would think these writers would have precise knowledge. The synoptics have Jesus and his disciples eating the last supper on a Friday, while John places it on a Thursday. As a result, in the synoptics, it is a Passover meal, while in John, it is eaten a day earlier and Jesus dies at the time when the Passover lambs were being

---

* Annie Jaubert, *The Date of the Last Supper* (Staten Island, NY: Alba House, 1965).

slaughtered. The existence of two calendars in Judaism at the time—the official lunisolar one at the Temple and the sectarian 364-day system of the Essenes—suggested the possibility that the synoptic writers followed one of these, and John, the other. Some found this solution attractive but it now enjoys less favor than it once did. There is, of course, no evidence elsewhere that these two systems were followed by the writers, nor is there any indication that Jesus himself might have preferred one calendar over the other. Moreover it is clear that John has a larger theological purpose in his passion section. The meal is not emphasized as a sacrament, foot-washing and mutual love are the highlights, bread and wine are not even mentioned in John's account of this last supper. And Jesus himself becomes the Passover lamb of his people.

While on the topic of sensational proposals like this, I should mention the suggestion made some 15 years ago that a few small papyrus scraps from Cave 7, a cave in which Greek texts have been found, were actually copies of New Testament books—Mark, Acts, Romans, 1 Timothy, James and 2 Peter. Naturally if that were true, the standard scenario for Qumran would have to be altered appreciably. What in the world are Christian texts doing in these caves? There remain some advocates of this position today but it has been largely abandoned on the grounds that too little of the texts is preserved and even for what exists, the correspondences with the texts in question are not exact.

But there are numerous points of contact between the Qumran documents and the text of the New Testament. In the scrolls for the first time we have the Semitic equivalents of some key expressions in the Greek New Testament—expressions like the "righteousness of God," "works of the law," "church of God" and so on. While such facts seem minor, they at least illustrate the deep roots of New Testament language in Semitic soil, something that has not always been sufficiently recognized. Also, that mysterious character Melchizedek of the Epistle to the Hebrews [7:1-17] has shown up in an important Qumran text where he plays a superhuman role. He is a kind of angel, who makes for interesting comparisons with Hebrews.

In connection with biblical interpretation, I think we have in the New Testament some examples of exegesis that would have appealed to an Essene of the sort we have at Qumran. At least the same kind of method is used, that is, it is assumed that the text is speaking to the present time which is part of the last time, the end of days. An instructive example appears in the second chapter of Acts. On Pentecost Peter is trying to explain why what has happened is not the result of the disciples' being drunk in the morning, but was a miraculous giving of the Holy Spirit. He says it happened in the fulfillment of prophecy and he cites Joel 2:28, "This is what was spoken by the prophet Joel: And in the last days it shall be, God declares, that I will pour out my spirit upon all flesh, and your sons and your daughters shall prophesy, and your young men shall see visions, and your old men shall dream dreams" (Acts 2:16-17). That phrase "in the last days" should catch our attention. What Joel foresaw for the last days was, according to Peter in Acts 2, happening at this first Christian Pentecost. The Hebrew text of Joel, however, does not actually have the words "in the last days"; it reads "afterwards." In Acts 2, Peter seems to have derived it from the context. But like the Essenes, he applied an eschatological prophecy to the present—to his present—to a momentous event in the history of his community. There are plenty of other examples in the New Testament of this kind of interpretation. The two communities appear to have approached the Scriptures, at least at times, in the same way.

Finally, a note about messianism. Both the Essenes and early Christians had messianic faiths. Both associated messiahs with the end, but the Christians differed in holding that he had already appeared once and would be back.

An intriguing feature of the Essenes' messianic faith was that they looked to the arrival of two messiahs. As one of the texts, the Manual of Discipline, puts it, at the end there will arise a prophet and the messiahs of Aaron and Israel. There would be a priestly and a secular messiah, with the latter probably being of Davidic lineage. These two are present at a meal of bread and wine described in the Manual of Discipline. Now this obviously differs from the Christian belief that Jesus, the descendant of David, was the only Messiah, even though He would appear twice. Nevertheless, it should be remembered, that there are differing portrayals of Jesus and his work in the New Testament. The Gospels, with their genealogies of Jesus and their association of him with Bethlehem, lay stress on his Davidic descent, but the Epistle to the Hebrews presents him in another light. There he is a high priest of the heavenly sanctuary. The writer knows that Jesus is not from the tribe of Levi, so he gives Jesus a priestly lineage by attaching him to the superior order of Melchizedek. Thus, in the Gospels, Jesus is a Davidic Messiah while in Hebrews, he is a priestly Messiah. In this way, the work of the two Qumran messiahs is performed by the one complex Messiah of the New Testament.

Much more could be added but enough has been said to show that the scrolls illuminate much more brightly for us the Jewish soil out of which the New Testament and the early church grew. As with the subject of the Jewish parties and literature of the period, so with the New Testament: The scrolls have supplied intriguing material to make our knowledge more complete and probably to raise more questions.

Questions & Answers

What is your opinion of Professor Ben-Zion Wacholder's book on the Temple Scroll?

Professor Wacholder of Hebrew Union College in Cincinnati wants to date the Temple Scroll to an earlier time, not far from 200 B.C.E., and to connect it with someone named Zadok. The designation of the Qumran group as the "Sons of Zadok" would have a different explanation in that way. I really do not see the point; I have not been able to accept his arguments in that book. I think he dates the Temple Scroll considerably too early. He has to date some other texts to accommodate this as well. The Book of Jubilees he dates at a much earlier time. I think that the Temple Scroll could easily be defended as a text from Qumran, perhaps from the early years of it. It has been argued that it differs from some Qumran texts, but I really do think that it has the same calendar in it as the Qumran texts do and, of course, it spends a lot of time talking about a temple. There has been a lot of debate about what that temple is and how it relates to the present one and the future one. I do not think that Wacholder has carried the day. He is not very impressed by paleographical arguments and so on and prefers to find allusions in much later texts to rather obscure characters who may have lived around 200 B.C.E.

Is there a comprehensive summary of what all of these 800 Qumran books are?

There is a catalogue that is being drawn up right now (that is not yet available) of what texts exist and so on. A couple years ago, maybe three or four years ago—about 1985—the *Biblical Archaeologist* had a couple of articles which provided that kind of a survey and gave the numbers that I gave to you for some of these biblical texts. That was an attempt to give an overview of them. There may well be others that I am not aware of but that is a rather easily accessible one.

What is the biblical tradition of the Ethiopic or the Abyssinian Church in that it includes the Book of Jubilees in its biblical canon?

The Ethiopic Church was isolated from the rest of the Christian church for centuries. It has its own larger canon, which includes a number of works that are not in anybody else's canon of the Old Testament. It has been speculated that its canon may reflect a period in the early church when there was a lot of disagreement about this sort of thing, with one group having a larger Old Testament than another. We do not have any texts that argue the point (at least I do not know about them)—that argue why Jubilees should be included and why other people did not or things like that; but I am very grateful that they have included this book. We would not have the texts of First Enoch or Jubilees or a number of other works if this very ancient Christian tradition had not preserved them for us and had not preserved an earlier state of canonical development when the question apparently had not been decided uniformly in the early church.

Have any books of the Bible been amended or changed as a result of the scrolls?

If you look at any contemporary translations of the Bible into English, you will see in the footnotes a number of references to available Qumran texts and sometimes those readings are included. For the Revised Standard Version, the Old Testament of which came out (I think) in 1952, the translators had access to the Isaiah scroll and included 15 or 17 emendations from the Isaiah scroll in their translation. There are more in the New Revised Standard Version, and the translators had access to other biblical material from Qumran. So this is part of the source material that any translator has to use today, but it will be indicated in the footnotes if it came from one of these Qumran texts. There have been a number changes of that sort.

*T*he alphabet was invented only once. All other alphabets
are derived from that one—the Semitic alphabet. The Semitic
alphabet was soon adapted by other cultures, including the
Greek. Aleph, beth *became* alpha, beta *and the word "alphabet." Kyle McCarter wrote his doctoral dissertation on when
the Greeks borrowed the Semitic alphabet. He has also written
the distinguished two-volume commentary on Samuel for the
Anchor Bible. He has served as president of the American
Schools of Oriental Research and he is now the William
Foxwell Albright Professor of Biblical and Ancient Near
Eastern Studies at the Johns Hopkins University. His talk
today will be on a scroll that has already been published, but it
will illustrate the ongoing and exciting nature of scholarship.
He is going to talk about the Copper Scroll, which was originally published unorthodoxly and, some say, improperly by a
scholar (John Allegro) who somehow got hold of it. That
publication triggered prompt publication of the official edition
by the man to whom it was assigned (J. T. Milik). But the
nature of scholarship is that it is always improving. You never
say the last word on these things, so now Kyle is personally
working on re-editing the Copper Scroll. Some of the things
that he is finding, I am sure you will find as fascinating as I
do. —H.S.*

P. KYLE McCARTER, JR.

The Mystery of the Copper Scroll

THE COPPER SCROLL IS AN anomalous part of the story we are telling today. That is, it does not fit into any of the categories we have been discussing except that it is rolled up (or it was rolled up) and it came out of one of the caves. It is written in a language that is different from the language of any of the other scrolls. It is written in a script that is not like the script of any of the other scrolls. It is written on a material that is different. The other scrolls are leather, a few were written on papyrus, but this is on a sheet of copper. And its content has no parallel. That is, in content it does not resemble any of the other Qumran scrolls—or anything else, except pirates' treasure maps in Hollywood movies. It is an unusual phenomenon, an anomaly.

What I want to do today is report to you on the project I am involved in with the Copper Scroll. In the process of giving that report, I will also have occasion to describe something of the circumstances of the discovery of the Copper Scroll and the special problems it presented to those who first investigated it. I also hope that my report will provide you with an example of the kind of project that is cooperatively undertaken by the international academic community to improve our access

The Copper Scroll. *Unlike any other scroll found at Qumran, the Copper Scroll was inscribed on two rolls of almost pure copper. It was recovered from Cave 3 in a spot apart from the other scrolls in the cave. Obviously, the fact that the text was inscribed on copper signified its unusual importance. Whoever wrote it must have wanted it preserved longer than it was thought an animal-skin scroll would last. When discovered, the rolls were so brittle that they could not be unrolled; finally, scholars had to slice the scroll into strips to look inside.* Courtesy Israel Antiquities Authority

to materials and our understanding of them.

The first slide is a map of Palestine (see p. x). We are concerned with a triangle of land that extends roughly from Jerusalem over to Jericho and down to Qumran. As I will explain, there are dozens of geographic locations referred to in the Copper Scroll, and many of those locations seem to be within that geographic triangle.

The Cave 1 discoveries that Hershel described to you this morning were made in 1947. The process of exploration was interrupted, as he explained, by the war, so that in the early 1950s there were only two caves known to the scholarly community. But fragments of leather with writing on them were showing up regularly in the antiquities market, and it was clear that other caves had been found by the Bedouin. So in 1952 a major expedition was mounted. It was a joint expedition involving a number of different international institutions that were working in Jerusalem at the time, principally the École Biblique, the American School of Oriental Research and Jordan's Department of Antiquities. A survey was undertaken in a kind of loose cooperation with the Ta'amireh Bedouin, who knew the area best, and, as Hershel said, that resulted in the discovery of the rest of the 11 caves.

Cave 3, the first of the caves discovered in the survey, was the cave from which the Copper Scroll came. Other, more conventional, leather scrolls were also found in Cave 3, but in the back of the cave, off by themselves, were two rolls of copper. It later became clear that these were two pieces of one scroll, and that was the discovery of the Copper Scroll.

The Copper Scroll was very brittle. The scholars who found it could see that there was writing on the inside and one scholar noticed that the writing seemed to describe the hiding places of treasures of silver and gold! But the scroll could not be opened because it was so brittle. It would fall apart if one tried to unroll it, and the techniques being developed at that time for working with leather materials did not apply to copper. And so there was a great deal of discussion about what should be done with it.

Eventually, the Copper Scroll was taken to the University of Manchester and cut into slices with a saw. The idea was that since it could not be unrolled, it must be cut. It was cut into a series of slices, and in that way it was opened to be read. The photographs of the scroll taken at that time were not poor quality photographs for the mid-1950s, but they are very difficult to work with today. When the Copper Scroll was published, these photographs were reproduced on a grainy surface. It is frustrating to go to the publication volume and try to use the photographs to reconstruct the text. As a result people have been largely dependent over the years on the edition made by J. T. Milik, the scholar who published the text. His drawing is what most people use when they read the Copper Scroll.

A decision was made several years ago to republish and re-edit all of the Qumran scrolls that had already been published. The reason was that they had been published in a variety of places over a number of years. Many of the editions were out of date, and many improved readings had been established. Princeton University Press agreed to sponsor the project, and a large number of scholars were invited to work on the various manuscripts. I was asked to work on the Copper Scroll. At the time I assumed, quite mistakenly, that I would have to work from the existing photographs, because copper and bronze artifacts are subject to bronze disease, a particularly destructive form of oxidation.

Many bronze objects that have been out of the ground for very long have deteriorated badly. I had suffered from this problem before, working with texts of a quite different type. Those were texts incised in bronze tablets from the Middle Bronze Age in an undeciphered script

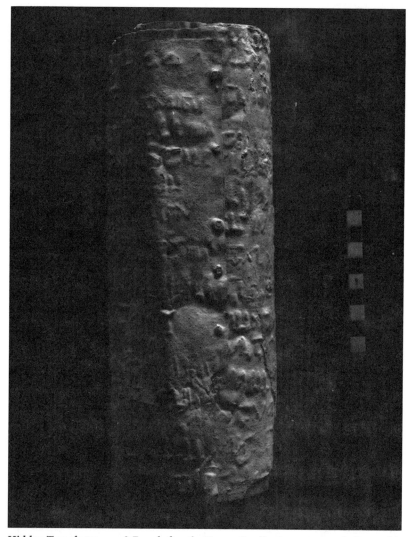

Hidden Temple treasure? *Even before the Copper Scroll was cut apart, scholars could see that the writing seemed to describe hiding places for silver and gold treasures. A set of rivets along the seam indicates where the two portions were originally attached. Judging from the Hebrew, the Copper Scroll was probably not written by a professional scribe, but by someone from a village who presumably wrote in a local dialect; this accounts for what seem to be misspellings and grammatical peculiarities. The Copper Scroll lists 64 locations, each followed by a quantity of valuables—mostly silver and gold, but sometimes priestly vessels. "In the funerary shrine of Ben Rabbah the Shalishite," we are told, are "100 bars of gold." Some speculate that the Copper Scroll might describe the location of the hiding places where the Temple treasures were taken to protect them from the Romans during the great Jewish revolt of 66 to 70 C.E.*
Courtesy Israel Antiquities Authority

The Copper Scroll, *now in the archaeological museum at the Citadel in Amman, Jordan, has been difficult to study because the photographs taken in the mid-1950s were poor judged by current standards. Until now most scholars had to rely on the photographs and drawings published by J. T. Milik, who originally edited the text. Now, Kyle McCarter is working on a new edition based on dramatic new photographs taken by specialists Bruce and Ken Zuckerman of the West Semitic Research Project in Claremont, California, who use the most advanced lighting and processing techniques.*
Bruce and Kenneth Zuckerman/West Semitic Research Project

used in the city of Byblos, the Greek name for the Phoenician Gebal—one of the most ancient cities in the Near East—located north of present-day Beirut. I managed to get new photographs of the Byblian texts and found that a high percentage of the surface had disappeared since their discovery. In short, they no longer exist, and I had assumed that the same was true of the Copper Scroll. After inquiring from people who knew about such things, however, I was delighted to find out that that is not the case.

The Copper Scroll is unusually pure copper—not bronze—and that apparently is one of the things that has protected it from bronze disease. It is not, however, in the same condition it was in 1952, or even in 1956 when it was cut up. There has been some deterioration; but in general, we still have the Copper Scroll. It did not disappear as it oxidized, and it is now on display in the Jordan Archaeological Museum. This is another way in which the Copper Scroll is anomalous. It is not in the Rockefeller, it is not in the Shrine of the Book. The vicissitudes of history were such that it has wound up in Amman. The Jordanians prize the scroll greatly, and they have it on display in a special case that was built for it in the 1950s.

After I learned these things, it became clear to me that what I needed to do first was to get new photographs. I could go look at the Copper Scroll (and I did that), but I knew I could not work from the Copper Scroll itself. Much of the work on the scrolls has to be done from photographs simply because the materials won't tolerate excessive handling. High quality photographs are an important part of the work anyone does with the scrolls. So my hope was that we could get new photographs using all the best modern techniques and the highest quality film available.

At this point I want to emphasize the point I made earlier about the importance of an international effort to work on a project like this. The purpose of the American Center for Oriental Research (ACOR)—the American archaeological center in Amman, Jordan—is to facilitate scientific projects in Jordan. Americans and people from all over the world use this center. The staff of ACOR has a close working relationship with the antiquities officials in Jordan and is in a position to facilitate projects. So ACOR was a crucial component of the team we put together for our photography project.

The director of ACOR at this time was Bert DeVries. Bert is a scholar and an archaeologist. He became the key to arranging this project to rephotograph the Copper Scroll.

The second person I need to tell you about as part of the project is Bruce Zuckerman. Bruce is a professor in the field we are all in.* That is, he is a scholar. But he is an expert photographer as well, and he has a brother, Ken, who is also an expert. Bruce has had a major project going on for years, photographing and rephotographing inscriptions—Dead Sea Scrolls, Phoenician inscriptions, all inscriptions from the region that we work in. Having developed techniques for photographing all kinds of materials, he was excited about the challenge to develop techniques for photographing copper.

Next to be mentioned is Dr. Ghazi Bisheh, the director of the Department of Antiquities of Jordan. We needed to work closely with him, so Bert went and talked to him, explaining what we wanted to do and asking about the department's interest in a new edition of the Copper Scroll. Dr. Bisheh was very supportive. He very much wanted to

---

* In addition to being an associate professor of religion at the University of Southern California, director of the West Semitic Research Project and of the USC Archaeological Research Project, Bruce Zuckerman is a preeminent photographer of ancient manuscripts. See also talk by James Sanders.

see this done, and his only requirement was that we should also attempt to develop a conservation portion of the project. Not only would we try to rephotograph the Copper Scroll, but we would also try to conserve it.

The agreement was that the photographs would be taken in December 1988. The photographs would be published first in the *Annual of the Department of Antiquities of Jordan* and then published as a volume in the Princeton University Press series on the scrolls. My job is to reestablish the text from the photographs—make a new edition, with a new English translation. A Jordanian scholar, Fawzi Zayadine, is making an Arabic translation so that there will be both English and Arabic translations of the new text.

The museum where the Copper Scroll is kept is up on the Citadel in Amman. Those who have visited Jordan know that the old part of Amman, the ancient capital, has a sharp hill in the middle of the modern city. On top of the Amman Citadel they have, appropriately enough, built the Jordan Archaeological Museum. The Copper Scroll is in a glass case along with a couple of fragments of leather scrolls. The individual pieces (slices) of the Copper Scroll itself are laid down on velvet-lined trays in the wooden box that was built for them.

The first step in the process was the removal of the individual trays from the case. The director of the museum supervised their move into a photography lab which the Zuckerman brothers had set up in the museum. I am not a photographer so I can't tell you about all the wonderful things that Bruce does. I can tell you the results are quite spectacular. In general what he does for this kind of material is take photographs with a very large negative, so that it can be enlarged almost infinitely without getting grainy. That obviously helps us: If the text keeps getting bigger and bigger, we can see it better and better. At the same time, 35 mm shots were taken to keep a record of the project, and a large number of Polaroid shots were taken. Bruce uses Polaroids to make sure that his main camera is going to show him what he is expecting to see. The lighting was set up, and the individual pieces of metal were photographed with spectacular results. The new color photographs are much easier to read than the black and whites taken in the 1950s.

Hershel alluded to the strange circumstances of the publication of the Copper Scroll. It was assigned to J. T. Milik but another member of the team, John Allegro, was very excited by the Copper Scroll and did not want to wait. He was an Englishman, and he went along to Manchester to be present at the opening. Allegro published his own edition two years before Milik's official edition came out.* Then Allegro went to Jordan and started looking for the treasure. It was one of those embarrassing episodes and aroused great consternation. The most

---

* John M. Allegro, *The Treasure of the Copper Scroll* (Garden City, NY: Doubleday, 1960).

A copper mosaic. *When the Copper Scroll was first photographed in the mid-1950s, a mosaic was made of the photographs by taking the original pictures of the sections, cutting them up and placing them to form a continuous column. This is column 9 of the Copper Scroll put together for* Discoveries in the Judaean Desert III, *ed. J.T. Milik, M. Baillet and R. de Vaux (Oxford: Clarendon, 1962), the official publication of the Dead Sea Scrolls.* Courtesy Israel Antiquities Authority

Sharper image. *Bruce and Kenneth Zuckerman rephotographed column 9, which is the equivalent of the top and bottom right sections on the mosaic. Note the set of rivet holes on the pointed part of the right edge. The clarity of this new photograph is astounding, especially as compared with the earlier photograph. Biblical Archaeology Society is grateful to Bruce and Kenneth Zuckerman of the West Semitic Research Project for allowing the reproduction of this never-before-available photograph.*

negative book review I have ever read was written about Allegro's book. It probably deserved it. Now Allegro, as idiosyncratic as he was, was a good scholar, but his edition is far inferior to Milik's. I think what happened was that Allegro rushed to get his version into print and consequently missed many readings that Milik was able to correct in his edition, which came out in the official series that publishes the Qumran scrolls.*

When working with inscribed materials it is important to have photographs taken with lighting from more than one angle. If light hits that incision in stone or metal from a particular angle, it will make the incision disappear. I have been fooled many times by having bad lighting or only one light angle. Normally, when Bruce photographs anything, he photographs from several light angles. That was not possible with the Copper Scroll because of the curved surface. Bruce could only light it from above and below, so he used two light angles on everything.

Let me say a little bit about the conservation project before I go back to our analysis of the scroll. The Copper Scroll is crumbling. The places touched by the saw in England exhibit an oxidation pattern. Centuries in the caves did minimal harm, but somehow the insult of the modern tool has started a process of deterioration along the cuts. Our biggest disappointment was when we first got the photographs back and began to compare them to the black and whites taken in the 1950s: On both sides of each saw cut, there has been a fair amount of material lost—in some cases up to a full centimeter. The Copper Scroll is slowly disappearing—and that has to be stopped. Also, there is a kind of crumbling around the edges and there are little pieces that have fallen down into the case. Bruce and I have approached conservation experts about this project and they now have a very important role in it.

What will conservation of the Copper Scroll mean? First of all, an expert in copper and bronze will have to go to Jordan and try to find some kind of treatment that will stop this oxidation process. Second, a new case must be made with special equipment to regulate the climate inside. Finally, if it turns out that the surface of the copper can tolerate it, we will make latex casts and from those casts make copies of the Copper Scroll which can be distributed to scholars.

Now let me list the peculiarities and problems in working with this text. It is written in Hebrew. It is a form of Hebrew that has a lot in common with Mishnaic Hebrew but it is not Mishnaic Hebrew. (The Mishnah is an early rabbinic text assembled in about 200 C.E.) In fact, it is unlike any Hebrew that we know, probably because this text was not

---

* J.T. Milik, "Le rouleau de cuivre provenant de la grotte 3 (3Q15)" in *Discoveries in the Judaean Desert III, Les 'Petites Grottes' de Qumran*, ed. Milik et al. (Oxford: Clarendon, 1962), pp. 199-302.

Conserving the crumbling Copper Scroll. *Here we see two of the three sections of the Copper Scroll in the Citadel museum in Amman. The museum case is opened and one section has already been removed for photographing. After centuries in a cave, a specially built case was nevertheless inadequate to prevent deterioration. McCarter discovered that, where the saw touched the copper, oxidation has occurred, and small pieces of the scroll have fallen down into the case. In some instances, as much as a full centimeter has been lost where the saw left its mark. Ghazi Bisheh, the director of the Department of Antiquities of Jordan, has therefore requested a joint conservation project to save the scroll from further deterioration.* Bruce and Kenneth Zuckerman/West Semitic Research Project

written by a professional scribe. It is probably a village dialect of Hebrew. This was a time when Aramaic speaking was the rule, but Hebrew was still spoken in villages, and so the author of the Copper Scroll, whoever he might have been, presumably wrote in his own dialect with all its idiosyncracies. To continue, the spellings of individual words are often peculiar. We know a variety of spelling systems, a variety of kinds of orthography, as it is called, from the various Qumran scrolls and from other manuscripts; but no orthographic system quite matches the one used in the Copper Scroll. Sometimes this seems to be because mistakes are being made. Other times it may be that it is not a spelling peculiarity but a grammatical peculiarity that we are not familiar with.

Next, the script is unusual. If you or I were to take a sheet of copper and attempt to write on it with a chisel or some other sharp

object, the result would be different from our normal handwriting. If
you were accustomed to writing with brush and ink on a piece of
leather, then your handwriting, when transferred to a metal surface,
would be even more distorted. In part, therefore, the handwriting is
peculiar because the scribe is working on an unfamiliar material, but
again it seems likely that this is not the hand of an expert scribe such as
those who wrote most of the leather manuscripts in the Qumran archive.

I n content, the Copper Scroll is a list of 64 locations. It has no introduc-
tion and no embellishment. It simply lists one place after another, usually beginning with a prepositional phrase ("In such and such a
place . . .") followed by one of the 64 locations; then a quantity of
valuables is given. Most of the hidden material is silver or gold. Some of
it, the part that is not silver or gold, seems to be items related to priestly
use—vessels of incense and similar things. But most of it is silver and
gold. The quantities are extremely large. They are unreasonably large.
They are listed primarily in terms of talents. There has been a lot of
discussion about the exact size of a talent at that time, and there is more
than one possibility; but even by the most conservative figure, we would
have truckloads of gold and silver here. It is a literally incredible amount,
and this immediately raises an issue that has to be discussed with respect to the Copper Scroll, namely, what on earth is it? That is, why in
the world did someone make this list?

Before I approach that question, let me offer some sample locations. The first location is in Herubah, or it might be Harobah. We
don't know which, and that immediately suggests what the problem is.
Herubah is probably a village. Either Herubah or Harobah would be a
good name for a village, but we are not told where Herubah/Harobah is,
except that it is in the valley of Achor. We do know where that is, so we
have a ballpark idea. "Beneath the steps that go to the east 40 cubits, a
chest of silver; its totality of weight is 17 talents." The second location is
"In the funerary shrine of Ben Rabbah the Shalishite, 100 bars of gold."
(One of my objectives in making a preliminary new translation was to
be very literal, trying not to be influenced by Milik, Allegro or any of the
others who have worked on the Copper Scroll.) The third location is
"On the mount of Kochlat," again a prominent place in the Copper
Scroll, but we don't know where the mount of Kochlat is. "Vessels of
incense with *login* [liquid measures of oil] and *ephods* [high-priest vest-
ments]"—you may recognize the priestly quality of these things. "The
totality of the incense and the hoard, several talents." The fourth location
reads: "From the mouth of the ruins of its door at the base of the
aqueduct from the north 6 cubits towards the cavity of the immersion."
It does not say what is there but it gives the partial location and then it
has three Greek(!) letters. One more example. "In the rubble pit of the

foundry of Manos," the foundry of a man named Manos or a village named Manos, "going down to the east 3 cubits up from the bottom, 40 talents of silver." The list goes on like that for 64 locations.

Many times the villages are places that are known or are mentioned several times. But as a rule, we don't know the names of the villages. It is possible to locate some places and that is the reason for thinking the sites are in that triangle of land that I began with. There have been proposals—a lot of them still reasonable—for some locations that are pretty far afield. Some of them lie to the north almost into Galilee; there are even a few on the east bank. Most of them, however, are either in Jerusalem itself or down the main wadi system that goes toward Jericho and on one of its branches toward the Wadi Qumran. So the locations that we can identify are in that general region.

Nowhere in the Copper Scroll is there the name of an individual who describes himself as being involved with the treasure or of someone to whom the treasure is entrusted. There are names of individuals as part of the place names. That is, private estates and private homes are mentioned, but not individuals. There also is no apparent legendary or mystical character to the Copper Scroll. If it is an imaginary treasure, it was imagined by someone who did not have too much imagination, because there is nothing really interesting about the text. The amounts of gold and silver are so large, however, that the question arises whether it was a real treasure or not.

Let me say again that the Copper Scroll is unique at Qumran. It is distinctive in all the ways mentioned earlier. Roland de Vaux,* who found it, seriously entertained the possibility that it did not have anything to do with the rest of the Qumran material, that it was hidden independently. After all, it was not in the same part of the cave as the other scrolls, and because of its unique characteristics, it does not have much in common with the other scrolls. Moreover, it is difficult to imagine that the Qumran community could have possessed such a treasure—it is such an enormous amount of wealth. Even if the members of the community were giving up their property to live a communal life, they would probably not have had all those bars of gold and silver to give. So the Copper Scroll treasure almost certainly has to be something like the treasure from the Temple in Jerusalem. In fact, almost everybody who works on the Copper Scroll thinks that is what it is. Many think that the treasure is imaginary, but most of those who think that it is imaginary think that it is imagining hiding places for the Jerusalem Temple treasures. Others think that it is not imaginary—that it was written on copper because the writer did not expect to get back soon and wanted

---

* Père Roland de Vaux was the excavator of Qumran and until his death in 1971 was editor in chief of the Dead Sea Scrolls.

the list of locations to be preserved. He never imagined that leather would last as it has in the caves; he considered leather a more perishable material than copper.

Let me mention one or two other things that connect the Copper Scroll with the Temple. First, it is difficult to imagine any other treasure that large in the country at the time. Second, there are references to priestly articles in the text as noted earlier. Third, there are some internal suggestions in the text. Consider, for example, location 32. Unfortunately this location is described in a fairly broken part of the text, on one of the edges. But it makes a reference to a treasure location in a cave on the property of "the House of Hakkoz," where there are supposed to be six bars of gold dug 6 cubits into the ground. The House of Hakkoz is interesting because that is a name we know. We know that if you go to the Bible and look at the names of the people who are involved with the reconstruction of the city of Jerusalem and its walls after the return from Babylonian Exile, you will find the Hakkoz family mentioned in the books of Chronicles, Ezra and Nehemiah. These biblical lists are arranged geographically, so that a group of families from one part of the country would work together on one particular part of the walls. The group of people with whom the Hakkoz family is listed are all people from the region around Jericho—in other words, the region that we are concerned with here. So it is likely that the House of Hakkoz of the Copper Scroll and the Hakkoz family mentioned in the Bible—who continued to be prominent in post-biblical times—are the same family. Moreover, according to the biblical evidence it was a priestly family. And more than that, it was the family that in the post-Exilic period was entrusted with the care of the Temple treasury! All this does not settle our question; but it does suggest that the Copper Scroll treasure, whether real or imaginary, is probably the Jerusalem Temple treasure. Either the Hakkoz family was involved because they still had some responsibility at this time for the Temple treasury, or their name was put in to give plausibility to this document.

Let me give you some conclusions. I have finished what I can do. I have a number of new readings, mostly based on the advantage of the new photographs. I still could not (and would not if I could) take you to the West Bank and show you any one of the locations. And if I could, I don't know what we would find there, because I don't know if this was real or imaginary treasure. I am persuaded that there is something we don't understand about the numbers, and so I continue to sympathize with those people who think that this is an imaginary treasure. The amounts of gold and silver and even the depths in which things were buried are too large. On the other hand, I am more persuaded by the very dullness of the document that it is probably not an entirely imaginary list. I think that this was a real list of something.

Questions & Answers

Why was the Temple treasury kept outside the Temple area?

The treasure would not have been kept outside the Temple area unless it needed to be protected because the Temple area was in danger. Well, the Temple area *was* in danger when the Romans came during the First Jewish Revolt, and we know from Josephus that Jews fled into the desert and hid their property. That's an age-old pattern—fleeing into that desert and hiding things in those caves—in different time periods. That's why it would not have been in the Temple. They thought in order to protect the treasure from the Romans, they had to hide it. The people who think this is a list of the Temple treasure think that it was divided up into several different places to protect it, and then this list was made.

Now, are there parallels to this? There really are not. There are other inscriptions that are on metal sheets. We have them in Hebrew, Phoenician, Aramaic, but they are not like this. They are sometimes prayers, sometimes temple dedications written on gold sheets and put up on the wall of a temple, but I do not know of a parallel to a metal text that is a treasure list.

Have there been any attempts to use modern computerization techniques to solve any of these problems?

There has been some of that kind of work. Some was done in the 1950s and 1960s. Obviously computers are more sophisticated now and it ought to be done again, but the particular part that seems to be promising in that regard is those mysterious Greek letters. Those have no known function. They do not correspond to any kind of abbreviation or numerical system that we have been able to establish. They seem to be some kind of secret code. They are Greek letters. They are not Hebrew letters, and the rest of the text is in Hebrew. Unfortunately, there are very few of them. There were six in the first few locations but there are not that many more in the whole thing. I would hope that some kind of computer program could be applied to those Greek letters and maybe figure what is going on there. It does seem to be some kind of code, but nobody has cracked that one yet.

*W*e turn now to the big question. The question everyone asks about Qumran. What effect does this enormous library have on the text of our Bible? That is going to be addressed by a very distinguished scholar who received his Ph.D. from Hebrew Union College. He was one of the people who was called in when the scrolls were found in the last cave, Cave 11. There was a Psalm Scroll, and Jim Sanders was called in to unroll that and to edit it and publish it. He has served as president of the major American organization of thousands of biblical scholars, the Society of Biblical Literature. He has been on the faculty of Union Seminary, and he held a joint appointment at Columbia. He is now on the faculty of Claremont Graduate School, and he is the founder of the Ancient Biblical Manuscript Center in Claremont, California, which has thousands of biblical manuscripts on negatives so that scholars can study them to see the variations in the biblical texts. In this archive is also a collection of photos of all the Dead Sea Scrolls, including the unpublished ones, but he can't let you see the unpublished ones because he is under a contractual agreement: When the negatives of the scroll photos were deposited there, he agreed not to allow anyone to see them except with the permission of the scroll editors, as we have discussed. He is a member of the United Bible Society. He served on the committee that has just put out the New Revised Standard Version of the Bible, and he has written 12 books including Torah and Canon [Fortess, 1972] and, his latest, From Sacred Story to Sacred Text [Fortress, 1987]. He is going to be awarded an honorary doctorate at Fribourg, Switzerland, next month. It is a pleasure to introduce him to you, James Sanders. —H.S.

JAMES A. SANDERS

Understanding the Development of the Biblical Text

WE SIMPLY HAVE TO ABIDE by all covenants and agreements that we have signed [referring to the agreement mentioned in the introduction], and we have done so in the case of the scrolls since 1980. A number of monasteries, abbeys, museums and the like put restrictions on the use of their materials; if we didn't abide by them we would have to close our doors and fold up. I think the scroll situation is going to change; indeed, it would change if the current head of the Israel Antiquities Authority would say that these agreements regarding access to the scrolls have been superseded. Then we would have no trouble.

I want to talk about our current understanding of the development of the biblical text because of the scrolls; as Emanuel Tov has recently written, it has been revolutionary. But before I do, I want to mention that we have a number of projects going on at the Ancient Biblical Manuscript Center; Bruce Zuckerman is involved in a good many of them. He is, as Kyle said, at the University of Southern California and runs his own shop there called the West Semitic Research Project which publishes a journal called *Ma'arav*. Zuckerman is also acting director of the Manuscript Center this year, and I am very happy about that. He comes out from USC one day a week to work with us. We are hoping to get the kind of funding that would permit us to have a full-time director. Most of the directors that I have had working with me have been my own doctoral students, because of lack of funding. But I have had some wonderful geniuses coming through to help with the Manuscript Center.

One of the things that Bruce has been doing is reformatting the negatives (that is, making new enhanced images) of our Dead Sea Scroll films; we have a foundation grant for that. The project has produced some remarkable results, so that we have set up a group of graduate students and others to read Zuckerman's reformatted negatives. We put the new negatives and positives on backlighting to see what different readings we might come up with because of the reformatting improvement. Now this is just improvement by photography—not digitizing. One of the negatives includes the upper left-hand corner of a second column of 1QSa [1Q28a: Règle de la Congrégation], a very troublesome passage, difficult to read. But with Bruce's work, now we can see that there is a superimposed text, and we can now read the two texts occupying the same space. We took that new film to Megavision in Santa Barbara, which has the best of these microdensitometers at the moment; they take a flashphoto of the film and bring it up in digitized form on a computer monitor. It is utterly remarkable what you can see.

Elisha Qimron, an Israeli scroll scholar, was with us when we went to Megavision in August. Qimron has remarkable eyes for reading this stuff, and he was astounded. Our practice when we see improved readings is to contact the editor of that scroll first to offer what we believe are improvements. Then, if the editor doesn't respond, or disagrees, we write again stating our intention to publish the new reading ourselves. But we would always contact the editor first. I think that is only fair.

Also in August I made contact for the first time with the national laboratories in Los Alamos. The government in the last three years has a new policy of technology-sharing with the private sector. The government and the national laboratories have control of what they share. They had never been asked by a nonprofit organization like ours to share their technology, wisdom and expertise, and they apparently need brownie points with nonprofit organizations. I think with their help we may be moving a little bit more rapidly towards digitizing than we thought.

One wants to be careful because they showed us at Megavision at Santa Barbara that you can actually move letters around in the manuscript shown on the screen. So we will never get away, I think, from having good photographic films to check against. I think that our vault, which maintains 60° Fahrenheit and 30 percent humidity will be the

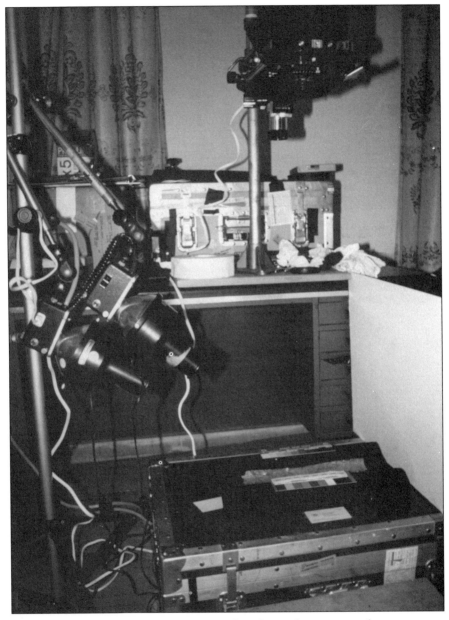

Preserving a precious legacy. *Bruce and Kenneth Zuckerman's arrangement for photographing the Copper Scroll includes two strobe flash units, on the left, one above the other. These spread a narrowly directed light across the complete scroll section lying on the black cloth in the lower right. A large white card stands behind the scroll to reflect the light back onto the scroll. The large format camera is above the scroll ready to take the picture.* Bruce and Kenneth Zuckerman/West Semitic Research Project tell, so to speak, where we can go and check the material just in case somebody manipulates the evidence to fit the grant application, so to speak.

There are a number of areas in which the scrolls have made an impact on our understanding of the period. Certainly one is that they have helped us to better understand the history of early Judaism. The field used to follow the George Foote Moore synthesis of there having been both a normative and a heterodox Judaism. But no longer.

Nearly everybody has called this group of people who lived at Qumran the Qumran *sectarians*, but that is shifting. Even Larry Schiffman—I was with him in a similar symposium last week at Siena College in Albany—even Larry is considering saying "denomination" instead of "sect," and I find that helpful.

The history of early Judaism has changed considerably. Michael Stone of Hebrew University, in a *Scientific American* article some 15 or 16 years ago, struck us all with the observation that now we cannot say normative or heterodox Judaism but rather we must speak of the pluriformity of early Judaism. Pluralism means one grants some truth to a position that is quite different from one's own; so we say pluriformity. The history of early Judaism is certainly marked by this pluriformity. We are learning now that there are any number of different kinds of early Jewish groups which produced the apocrypha and the pseudepigrapha that have been referred to in the course of the day. We have found new implications for the history of the period because of our rereading of all that material. James Charlesworth of Princeton, who has been mentioned a couple of times today, is editing with a former student of mine, Craig Evans, a volume on pseudepigrapha and the New Testament, which I hope will come out next year.

In a recent publication [*Discoveries in the Judaean Desert VIII, The Greek Minor Prophets Scroll from Nahal Hever*] edited by Emanuel Tov of Hebrew University [Jerusalem] and Bob Kraft of the University of Pennsylvania, Tov says that Dominique Barthélemy's thesis about the stabilization of the biblical text will always be known for its masterly treatment of this scroll and that his 1963 book* revolutionized biblical scholarship. I think that it has certainly changed our view of the history of the transmission of the text, which is what I would like to focus on now.

Where did the biblical text come from? I am often asked that question when I talk about the New Revised Standard Version. The NRSV is not *the* Bible; no translation is *the* Bible. So what is the Bible? What and whence these texts? We have thousands of manuscripts of the

---

* Barthélemy, *Les devanciers d'Aquila*, VT Sup 10 (Leiden: Brill, 1963), pp. 163-178.

two testaments. There are over 5,200 Greek New Testament manuscripts, no two of which are alike. They come from different areas and communities in antiquity and that accounts for some differences. There are also scribal goofs and errors. The earliest manuscripts we have of the Hebrew Bible and New Testament exhibit a limited amount of textual fluidity. Why is this the case? The hypothesis which I think best accounts for that is, first of all, that the portions that exhibit fluidity come after the Pentateuch, or the Torah—though there is some fluidity there—beginning with the early prophets, the latter prophets and certainly the Writings. They had not reached the kind of authoritative status that we now call canon for such groups. But more than that, ancient tradents [that is, traditionalists, scribes, copyists or translators] served their communities. They did not copy something, or translate something, just because they had a sabbatical leave and time on their hands! I think that the old, unexpressed image of biblical scholarship for the past 200 years has been that the evangelists and other writers of the Bible were like professors in their universities with sources in front of them to copy, some from this source and some from that source. The tradents worked to serve their communities; they wanted their people to understand this material.

Early manuscripts were written to be read to the community. Most early Christians were illiterate. Most people were illiterate. Literacy of the sort that we know today, particularly reading in silence, has only become common in the last couple centuries. The few literate folk in ancient communities would share their skills and read aloud for all the community, then they would all come to some kind of community understanding. We inherit this culture of orality in worship services today—Jewish and Christian—in the oral reading of Scripture in worship each week. One might ask why the pastor or the priest or the rabbi could not ask the congregation to take a copy of the Bible out of the pew rack and, while an anthem is being sung, read the passage of the day individually and silently. There is a mighty flowing stream of orality with regard to Scripture. It is read aloud as a community experience. Tradents wanted their communities to understand, so they would slightly alter the text to facilitate understanding.

You saw flashed on the screen today several texts from the scrolls from the caves in which there were no vowel points and no accent marks; also you saw no *Masorot*—lateral or marginal notations by scribes—as will be the case when we get to the early medieval and perhaps the later ancient biblical manuscripts copied by the Masoretes.

There developed in Judaism a movement of stabilization of the biblical text from those early examples of relative or limited fluidity we have been discussing. Moshe Greenberg was the first actually to write on this but it was picked up by Barthélemy. Barthélemy discovered that the Greek Minor Prophets Scroll from Nahal Hever is a revision of the older Greek translation of the minor prophets rectifying it toward the proto-Masoretic text that we can now describe from the discovery of the scrolls. The earliest scrolls do seem to exhibit some relative fluidity.

There have been theories about how to account for that. Text critics tend to want to talk about families of texts, so that is standard in text criticism and there are those, such as our colleague at Harvard, Professor Frank Cross, who believe they see families of texts—Babylonian, Palestinian and Egyptian. Most scholars do not see that as clearly as Frank does, but nonetheless we all have to observe this relative fluidity.

The history of the transmission of the text due to what Barthélemy did, following Moshe Greenberg, includes four periods of text transmission. The first period is that of the Ur-text and is not the province of text criticism, but rather of historical and literary theory; it attempts to reconstruct what Amos or Isaiah really said, or should have said. The second period was that of relative fluidity. The third period was that of pronounced and exceptional stability, even proto-Masoretic stability. The fourth is the period of the Masoretic text. Between the relative fluidity of the second period and the relative stability of the third period was a remarkable development. The Greek Minor Prophets Scroll shows pretty clearly to all who have studied it that one of its major purposes was to rectify the older Greek translations by bringing them closer to the developing proto-Masoretic text. Tov says that the scroll depends on the Septuagint and revises it toward a Hebrew text close to the Masoretic text. It is moving in the direction that we will know by the end of the first century of the Common Era of Aquila, Symmachus and Theodotion in Origen's *Hexapla.* The period of stabilization is demonstrable. The United Bible Society's Hebrew Old Testament Text Project, of which I have been a member for 21 years now, and the Hebrew University Bible Project (HUBP)—started in the early 1950s to edit the Aleppo Codex,* which was taken to Jerusalem from a synagogue in Aleppo, Syria—both subscribe to the same revised fourfold history of text transmission. According to Moshe Goshen-Gottstein, the Aleppo Codex dates to a time earlier than the oldest complete Hebrew manuscript that we have—the Leningradensis in the library in Leningrad. It dates to 1005 and Moshe Goshen-Gottstein dates the Aleppo Codex to 915, nearly a century earlier.

The first period was that of the Ur-text or the originals. We are now very careful about using the word "original," because we don't really know what we mean by it. You may know far better what we should mean by that than we do. Recently Emanuel Tov, Martin Jan Mulder and others have dealt with this. Do we use the word "original"

---

* Harvey Minkoff, "The Aleppo Codex," *Bible Review,* forthcoming.

Biblical text fluidity. *This leather fragment from the Greek Minor Prophets Scroll demonstrates that in the early development of Judaism biblical texts were not stable. The Greek Minor Prophets Scroll is a revision of an older Greek translation of the minor prophets. The author/scribe who worked on this, probably between 50 B.C.E. and 50 C.E., made revisions toward the Hebrew proto-Masoretic text. This manuscript, found in a nearby wadi, differs from the Qumran texts because it is written almost entirely in Greek. Only one word—the tetragrammaton yod* heh vav heh *or Yahweh—appears in Hebrew, at the lower left corner and at the left, six lines from the bottom. Yet it is written not in the square Aramaic Hebrew script usually used at the time the scroll was written, but in the older paleo-Hebrew script, used before the sixth-century B.C.E. Babylonian Exile.* Discoveries in the Judaean Desert VIII (Clarendon Press, 1990).

or do we just drop the word because we do not have autographs of anything? We have only apographs [copies]. That throws the focus back on the communities again. They were copied for whom? They were copied for what reason? They were copied for communities of faith, in Judaism and Christianity. Therefore, we have to say that we don't really know exactly the inception of any of these texts, but they develop into what we call traditioning process. Then the various parts of the Bible became important enough to various believing communities that they were copied more accurately, which starts in the end of the first century B.C.E. and culminates in a remarkable way at the end of the first century and the beginning of the second century of the Common Era.

We are not really sure as to why it came about. I think it would have been because of sociopolitical reasons. I suggested in an article in a journal a decade or so ago that it was probably because of the need of Judaism to meet the Hellenistic crisis and all that meant. The Torah, or Pentateuch, was in effect quite stable from the late fifth century B.C.E. Torah was Judaism and Judaism was Torah and all that developed out of that including Oral Law (the Talmud). A relatively stable, or frozen, text of laws dating from the Bronze and Iron Ages meant that you have a bunch of laws for which you don't have problems and a bunch of problems for which you don't have laws. It was a progressive process as Judaism began to see the need to work out Oral Law from the stabilized text of Torah. The move was from sacred story, which is always adaptable, to sacred text which is considerably more stable. The same thing happened with the nationalization of Christianity in the early fourth century C.E. where earlier texts were relatively fluid but there began to be accurate copying when Constantine became a Christian, and later when Christianity became the official religion.

If one looks then at the biblical materials from Murabba'at and then those from Masada and others that could date from the Second Jewish Revolt against Rome (132-135 C.E.), those are proto-Masoretic texts and amazingly stable. They read for the most part the way this Leningradensis manuscript—which is the earliest complete Hebrew Bible—reads. That remarkable stabilization continued for the Septuagint after Aquila and Theodotion in Origen's work in the *Hexapla* and later in the works of Jerome who carried on Origen's idea of *Hebraica Veritas*. Now why is this interesting? Because the First Testament of the early church, was the Septuagint, or Greek translations of the early Jewish literature—Torah, Prophets, Writings and in many cases Apocrypha and some Pseudepigrapha.

This brings up, of course, the question of canon which Jim VanderKam addressed this morning. I agree with his remarks in this regard. Whenever one says canon, one has to be clear which community one is talking about. If one says canon, one has to say which canon. There are many canons. The Ethiopian Orthodox canon has 81 books in it. I was talking to the Armenian Archbishop of Jerusalem, who is working with Michael Stone of Hebrew University on a corpus of Armenian manuscripts. He came to visit the Manuscript Center, and I said that I could not remember if the Armenian canon includes Fourth Maccabees, and he said they have only First, Second and Third Maccabees. The Jewish canon is the smallest, the next is the Protestant, then the Roman Catholic and finally the various Eastern Orthodox communities. Professor VanderKam said this morning that we don't really know the limits of what would have been thought of as authoritative traditional literature at Qumran. Was Jubilees authoritative for them? We do

The Aleppo Codex. *Dating to 915, according to Moshe Goshen-Gottstein of the Hebrew University Bible Project, the Aleppo Codex is the finest and oldest relatively complete Masoretic text of the Hebrew Bible. The Masoretic text—named after a group of scholars called Masoretes who standardized the text in the tenth century—contains vowels, cantillation marks and accents. Until the discovery of the Dead Sea Scrolls, the Aleppo Codex was the oldest nearly complete Hebrew manuscript of the Bible. In 1947, some sections were destroyed in a pogrom against Aleppo's Jewish community. The remaining leaves were subsequently smuggled from Syria to Jerusalem. The page shown here is the text of 1 Chronicles 2:26-3:4. The Masoretic marks appear above and below the lines and in the margins.* Hebrew University Bible Project not find the word canon at this period, but was it approaching some kind of authority such as the Torah already had? We don't know. It is very difficult to say. I am pretty clear in my mind that the Psalter they had at Qumran was not yet closed. For instance, we always say we have 150 Psalms. I don't know if you have looked at Leningradensis or not, but the last psalm in it is numbered 149; so 150 psalms is simply what you say if you want your gold star in Sunday school.

We can see the development of the text toward stability, from the kinds of consonantal manuscripts you saw this morning to Leningradensis. Here is a photograph of a leaf from Leningradensis which a team from the Ancient Biblical Manuscript Center just photographed in Leningrad in May and June. We sent a four-person team to Leningrad to photograph the codex in the Saltykov-Shchedrin State Public Library. We were the first foreigners ever permitted to photograph that collection. They have been more open because of *glasnost*, but even more so because of poverty in the Soviet Union now.

You saw manuscripts this morning with just consonants and maybe a few marginal notations, but the Masoretes did three things with those consonants. They inserted vowels according to the tradition of the oral readings of the time. They inserted accent marks (*te'amim*) and cantillation marks (in the case of the poetic sections) so the lector knows where to pause, how to parse a sentence and so on. Hershel was citing from Isaiah 40 this morning, "A voice cries: 'In the wilderness prepare the way of the Lord' " is the way the Masoretes put the accent marks. Matthew was free to read the verse in his way because he did not have the advantage of these Masoretic accent marks. He was able to say "A voice cries in the wilderness: 'Prepare the way of the Lord,' " and apply it to John the Baptist.

They put the *Masorot* in the lateral margins and in the top and bottom margins. These were notations by scribes to subsequent generations of scribes for copying accurately. I sometimes have called these sentinels, or soldiers, in the margin to protect the transmission of the text now that it is stabilized. Martin Jan Mulder contends that the stabilization process still continues. I sometimes think that one of the ways it is continuing is that we now have photography and Xerography and that sort of thing. The scribal notations in the margin relate to words in the text opposite it that have *circelli*, or white faced circles, over them. The most frequent notation is a Hebrew letter *lamed* with a dot over it; this is an abbreviation of the Aramaic word meaning "there is no other, it is unique as written," so the scribe knows that that form with its vowels and its consonants is the only time it ever appears in the Hebrew Bible, and he must not make a second one. And sometimes it will have a *bet*, which means that that word, just that way, appears twice in the Hebrew Bible.

Leningradensis. *Dating to 1005, Leningradensis, or Leningrad codex, is the second oldest Masoretic text of the Hebrew Bible and has been used as the standard for critical editions of the Hebrew Bible. This photograph, taken in the Leningrad state library where the text is housed, was made by Bruce Zuckerman for the Ancient Biblical Manuscript Center. The 982 leaves of Leningradensis contain corrections and erasures, an indication that it was revised, perhaps in accordance with the Aleppo Codex or a similar manuscript. Pictured is folio 40a showing the end of Exodus 14 and the beginning of the Song at the Sea, Exodus 15. The most frequent notation is the Hebrew letter* lamed *with a dot over it, an abbreviation of the Aramaic word meaning "there is no other," indicating that this is the only time the word appears in the Bible.* Bruce and Kenneth Zuckerman, West Semitic Research Project

These people knew the Bible by heart. They did not have television or paperbacks and the Olympiad was held only once every four years! They did not have means of referring to other passages by chapter and verse numbers; that comes later. They referred to a passage by just a few select words and they knew exactly where that passage was. Where we have doublets in the Bible, such as Psalm 18 and 2 Samuel 22 [David's Song of Thanksgiving], or the two sets of Decalogues (in Exodus 20 and Deuteronomy 5) and so on, as often as not there are words that are different. The discrepancies have a notation in the Masoretic column: "Keep the difference" was the message. "Keep the discrepancies, keep the anomalies, keep what seems to you a contradiction. Don't harmonize. That is dangerous. Whatever you do, don't harmonize." Where there are doublets and triplets, integrity is maintained.

Here is a "carpet page" [decorative pages that look like Oriental carpets] from Leningradensis which we just photographed [color plate v]. We at the Manuscript Center have been working with the Leningrad library for some ten years; we have acquired materials on microfilm during that time, usually through barter. At the time they preferred to have books from Israel, which they couldn't otherwise get. We had a decade-long relationship with them, especially with Viktor Lebedev, the head of the Semitic Division of the library. Then three years ago we began to send people over. People like Professor Stanislav Segert, and others who were going over anyway, talked to them in the library about what we wanted to do. We decided that our first project should be sending a photographic team over to do something where political heads would not roll, and that it would be safe to photograph this Leningradensis manuscript because it has already been published. Not only has it already been published, it is the basis of most critical texts of the Hebrew Bible that we have. No foreigner had ever been allowed to go photograph something in the library. You could take a picture of your spouse on the steps or something like that to show you'd been there, but nobody had been permitted to work on the collection. We had to make a proposition that would fly. That did not bring the invitation we needed; so we kept probing and it was suggested that gifts would be in order. You should have seen what they took with them to Leningrad. Finnair agreed finally to take the equipment without extra charge, but that was before they had seen how much it was actually going to be—36 huge cartons. They honored the agreement going over, but not for the return trip. We smiled because we knew we would not bring much back except the developed film. We were going to leave the rest as gifts. We left them fine photographic equipment and a lot of film, and now they are asking us to come back and teach them how to use it.

Somebody has recently said that the Soviet Union is a Third World country with immense atomic power and I think that is very apt. Our team would not have had food if it had not been for Viktor and Svetlana Lebedev. Mrs. Lebedev had them to dinner every evening, or they would not have had dinner. She also provided them with breakfast; they were able to get a bite of lunch at the museum dispensary. It was all very difficult and we think that they did an excellent job. Bruce Zuckerman's photographs are brilliant. We are negotiating now with publishers in Jerusalem to have them published; you will then be able to see how much better they are than those that were published by Makor in 1971 from microfilms.

By the way, they found no photographic equipment in the library. All they had in the library was a microfilm machine, and it is really ancient. We will always be known as the first photographic team to get in to work in the library, but we see ourselves as door openers, gate openers and not gatekeepers. We don't want to hold anything to ourselves. But if you do want to make a proposal to the library, be sure that you think of gifts because they are very needy. Their collection is well taken care of and whatever else one might say about the economy, the library is kept very clean and very orderly. This is a picture of a carpet page that you don't see in the Makor edition. It is actually the signature of the scribe—"I am Samuel, the son of Jacob. I wrote the consonants and inserted the vowel points and the Masoretic notes." That is the signature page. In our last appeal letter, incidentally, we are offering, to any donors who will give $200 or more to the Manuscript Center, a life-sized copy of that page.

Martin Jan Mulder says the stabilization of the text is not yet finished, and I think that is right. The stabilization of the text continues, and that is part of what text criticism is about. The question then becomes at what stage do you aim in the transmission of the text to arrive at a critically responsible text. It is not easy to answer. We cannot go for the "original" as we once thought. Tov, Jan Mulder and Barthélemy all agree on that point and I think I do, too. Now that doesn't mean that I don't want to try, as a literary historical critic, to try to reconstruct what was first said or written, but when we are deciding what text to arrive at, we just say the most responsibly critical text that we can get, whether it is the Masoretic text, an earlier Hebrew reading or the Septuagint, and that has to do with early understandings of canon. At what point in the history of transmission of the text should we look for establishing a critically responsible text? That is always a question which is a part of the continuing stabilization process.

The interface between text and canon is important to keep in mind. The question then becomes whether or not we should really pillage one type of text to correct another. There are those who say that we should try to go back behind proto-Masoretic and pre-Masoretic and the Septuagint to still an earlier period; but some now disagree with that. If we don't have any "satisfactory" reading in any witness at all, we still should not reconstruct the text; reconstructing would eliminate conjectures. Conjectures are always changing in scholarship anyway. Look at the conjectures about what a text ought to have been just within this century. All one has to do to witness textual fluidity today is to get down the various editions of the Bible one has at home. Compare the King James with the RSV, and those two with the NRSV, and those three with the New Jerusalem Bible and so on. You will get a feeling for the kind of textual fluidity we are talking about. If that is not sufficient, just go to church next Sunday to hear how adaptable the text is.

One of the ideas that I am toying with in my own thinking is that it may now be time to honor the several traditions that we receive. Instead of attempting to pillage the Septuagint to correct the Masoretic text, or the like, we might translate both where there are doublets, or two versions, as with the Ten Commandments. For instance, the story of Hannah in 1 Samuel 1, as Stanley Walters has recently shown, is a good bit different from the story of Anna in 1 Kingdoms 1 of the Septuagint, though it appears to be basically a translation of the Masoretic text. If one doesn't focus just on sentences and phrases but looks at the whole of the text, the full context, each has its own conceptuality and its own integrity. In the Masoretic text, the focus is on Hannah. In the Greek text, the focus is on her husband; and that would appear to be a cultural difference.

Just recently I was comparing the four annunciations in Genesis 15, 16, 17 and 18. Genesis 15 is a modified annunciation form telling Abraham he will have a son. The passage starts with Abraham's complaint to God that God had promised him progeny but now he is too old and still childless. He asks what God is going to do about it. In very interesting places the Septuagint refers to the man—as in one place in Genesis 17 where God promises Abraham will indeed have a son from her, meaning Sarah, the Septuagint has masculine suffixes in those instances. I don't think that indicates a different *Vorlage*, I think that a tradent was serving his or her community; and that community would probably have been a Hellenistic one in which the organization of the household with the man as the master over women, children and slaves was very clear, and even more macho perhaps than in the comparable Semitic societies.

I have dreamt of a Bible with translations of both versions into English. I wonder if lay folk would accept a Bible where there are doublets of this sort. The story has its own integrity in the Masoretic text, but its "translation" has its own integrity in the Septuagint. Why not let the faithful have them both? There might be one translation on the top half of the page and the other on the bottom half of the page. I think that it is time for us to stop fooling the people, making them think that there is just one Bible and that *our* Bible committee got closer to it than *their* committee did. Rather it is time, I think, to celebrate the riches that we have where there are such doublets, as in the story of David and Goliath. The Bible already has doublets in the Hebrew text, many doublets— Psalm 18 and 2 Samuel 22, the two sets of Ten Commandments, and so on— and their differences are to be kept. It seems to me that it ought to be possible for us to have translations for the faithful that can witness to other ancient points of view of familiar accounts. Must we continue to pretend that only our group is right denominationally and others are not right, and it is just too bad about others?

After all, the Revised English Bible and the NRSV have the Hebrew Esther in the so-called canonical section and the full Greek Esther— all of it in its full integrity—in the Apocrypha. Because Jerome wanted the true Hebrew translated for the Catholic Bible in Latin he put the additions to Esther and Daniel in the back and called them "Addenda." If you read the Greek of Esther, and compare it with the Hebrew of Esther, each has its own integrity with its many, many small little differences, as well as the larger "pluses" throughout. A doctoral dissertation has recently compared the three major Greek forms of Esther with a structural analysis of each, and each has its own points to make and its own conceptuality and integrity. The Hebrew text is still in the process of standardization, but I wonder if it would not be proper for there to be an effort afoot to provide our people with the differences where they exist and let them see that there have been differences all along. I have been told by some that that would just destroy the Bible because lay folk still want to think of the Bible as somehow "inerrant." The truth of the matter is that all biblical passages have been community property almost from the first repetition. It may well be that if there should ever be the possibility of discussing the text of Isaiah with Isaiah, he might very well say, "But I did not say that." It has nonetheless become community Isaiah property and he might just have to live with it.

Questions & Answers

What connection does the Leningrad Codex have with the Masoretic text that's in every Torah in every synagogue?

The Leningrad Codex is the basis of current critical editions of the Hebrew Bible. . . . I just found out last week by a telephone call from

Malachi Beit-Arieh, the director of the National Jewish Archives, who had just returned from Leningrad—he did not do any photographic work there but was permitted to look through the collection—that there are 2,500 codices of the Hebrew Bible there dating before 1100. I said, "Say that again." He said, "Yes, you know we thought there were 30 or 31 manuscripts of the Hebrew dating before 1100?" I said "Yes." He said, "There are 2,500." I said, "Malachi, 2,500?" He said "Yes." Now there are 982 of these leaves in the Leningradensis including the carpet pages. Beit-Arieh said of those 2,500 codices there are some that have as few as 30 but some as many as 1,000 pages. On some of them the Masoretic notations are quite primitive so that he thinks that we may now be able to rewrite the history of the development of the Masorah, and the Masoretic contributions to the text, because now we will be able perhaps to line them up in a certain historical development. That is astounding. Our cataloguer from the Manuscript Center is in Leningrad now working in the collection. So we should know more soon. Beit-Arieh is going back over in January to do microfilming. We need a catalogue and index of the whole collection. It is a little bit like discovering Qumran Cave 12. To me it is just astounding.

The Leningradensis is the text that dates to 1005 and is the basic text for all critical editions of the Hebrew Bible. Now what you have in synagogue, the traditional text, is the Second Rabbinic Bible. The stabilization process had several stages. Jacob ben Hayyim published in the early 16th century what we call the Second Rabbinic Bible, which was very different from the First Rabbinic Bible. Then that printed edition became standard for all Ashkenazi Jews. Now what you have in synagogue may be the traditional text, that is to say the Second Rabbinic Bible.

Have any of the findings of the Dead Sea Scrolls been incorporated into these newer versions of the Bible?

Professor VanderKam answered a similar question this morning. If you look in your Bible in the marginal notes at the bottom (sometimes they are in italics) you see noted how other authorities or other manuscripts read, and Q is used to indicate a Qumran reading. It indicates what has been learned from the scrolls. One thing is this Hannah story I was just talking about. The NSRV melds the two versions in the old manner and at the very end of that, the NRSV says that Hannah left the child at the Temple. Now, what is the basis for that statement? It is a lacuna in 4QSam^a that ends with a suffix, "him." Professor Cross conjectured that what was in the lacuna was, "She left him there," and so the NRSV reads. No other Bible has that. That is an example. You also have a place elsewhere, I think somewhere in Kings, where you have three or four verses that are quite, quite different in the scrolls from what they are in the Masoretic text and the NRSV uses the Qumran version. There are a number of instances where NRSV readings are significantly influenced by the scrolls.

Panel Discussion

Would the scholars please comment on the problem of scroll publication? Hershel Shanks' point of view is that it's not getting done fast enough. Perhaps they would talk about why that may be.

Hershel Shanks: I think I will exercise one of my prerogatives as chairman to reply to the "gadfly" charge (made against me by the questioner)—mostly by way of what lawyers call "confession and avoidance." I confess to being a gadfly, but I want to make it clear that, as I tried to state in my criticisms, I believe the scholars are conscientious, brilliant, fine people. I also did not have a chance to answer publicly a question often raised at meetings like this—the question that someone raised with me at the intermission—whether there might be a religious or doctrinal or political reason that the scholars are keeping these things secret. It is impossible to prove this one way or the other, but it is my firm conviction that there is no such intent, that this has nothing to do with the slow pace of publication.

Second, I want to make it clear that I have not criticized the scholars for taking time, as much time as they need. My criticism is directed at their refusal to let others see the scrolls. I have not called for the scholars to hurry up their work; I have called for the release of photographs so that other people can see the scrolls. As a matter of fact, a philanthropic foundation has offered $100,000 to publish the photographs, and the scroll editors have refused to do this. So my criticism of the scholars is not that they are slow, but that they are monopolists. And with that introduction, I will leave my three colleagues to respond.

James VanderKam: I think that is a helpful clarification of what has been the point of your criticisms. I can perhaps just stress that work with these fragments, especially the fragmentary texts, is extremely time-consuming and difficult. In the work that I am doing I just have a small amount of material, relatively speaking. It covers just 11 plates. Jozef Milik has hundreds of plates and naturally that must seem like a very large burden after a while, even though he has done a lot of work on them. I had assumed that I would finish up my work very quickly, but as I have gotten into it, I have discovered it takes a long time. Once I think I have a problem solved, the next day I look at it, and it may look different.

It is wonderful when I can compare the later translation of the book, the Ethiopic one, with the Hebrew fragment, and discover that they line up very nicely; when I translate the Ethiopic back into the Hebrew and it fits the available space between the Hebrew bits and pieces. But that does not always happen, and it can be trying to sort out the fragments. It takes time. Part of the reason I showed some of the slides that I did—showing you those very small fragments—was to arouse sympathy in the audience, to show that they are not very easy to work with. You can always raise the question, do these little, tiny things that have just a letter or two on them really belong there or are they something else?

But I agree entirely. Time-consuming as it is, it does not take 40 years. Really it would have been wiser to say that a certain team has the right to the scrolls for a while, and they should seek out the advice of their fellows—which they did. But after a certain amount of time, it should be opened up to a wider group of scholars—and this is finally happening now.

Shanks: We are supposed to talk with each other a little bit up here, so I am going to try to pinpoint an issue, Jim [VanderKam]. It seems to me that you answered a question or criticism that I really didn't make and you failed to answer a criticism that I did make. You explained why it is so difficult to edit these texts and why it takes so much time. And then went on to say that it is taking too much time. I agree with that 100 percent, both ends of that. It is difficult. I don't want to minimize that in the least. But sometimes the answers to my criticism, answers like yours, seem to imply that I have no understanding of the difficulty. I do appreciate the difficulty. I concede that to you, but my narrower point is that after 35 or 40 years, let other scholars see the scrolls. Let them see the photographs, that is the criticism which I don't think you answered.

VanderKam: I agree entirely and that is why I show my material to others. Anybody who wants to help me may, if they can see better things on them. I think it should be a communal effort, and I think the scrolls should have been thrown open to a wider group of people long ago.

Shanks: I might say by way of background that this same thing happened with another scroll, the Gospel of Thomas from the collection called the Nag Hammadi codices. This scroll too was assigned to a team of scholars who wanted to write a long commentary. But the scroll was kept in the Coptic Museum in Cairo and the director of the Coptic Museum went ahead and published photographs of the Gospel of Thomas. It was a terrible edition. But, nevertheless, based on this, scholars all around the world looked at the photographs and they made Latin and Swedish and English and Finnish and French translations. This encouraged the team that had been assembled to publish their own translation. So we have a little precedent for what can be done. I don't understand the reluctance of the scholars to let others see the photographs and say, as you said, Jim, let's get all the help we can.

Kyle McCarter: When the issue is discussed within academic circles, it becomes a volatile issue. It is important to remember that we are not talking about the Dead Sea Scrolls alone. There is a serious problem with archaeological publication of all kinds. Many times the reasons are personal and involve individuals. Many times you know why a particular inscription has not been published because you happen to know the particular scholar that was supposed to do it. And because there is this very long tradition which says that someone who finds something is supposed to publish it or give it to someone else to publish, scholars continue to be personally involved. It becomes very important to Professor so-and-so, if he has a new Aramaic inscription to publish, that he should be able to do that, and he takes it very seriously, becomes very emotionally involved with it. Then when time goes by and something does not get published—I have in mind a couple of specific examples that have nothing to do with scrolls—the scholar feels bad. Maybe he cannot read it. I know in one case an inscription was assigned to a poor man who simply could not read it, though he was supposed to be a great scholar. He finally bit his tongue and published it, and then everybody realized that nobody else could read it either. You have to realize that he was afraid of destroying his career by publishing that. Sometimes these issues are personal. They are emotional and they involve human individuals. That is why it is very easy to agree with the principle that there is no excuse for things going 35 or 40 years, while at the same time feeling protective towards some of the people that are guilty.

Shanks: I want to interrupt. Here's a man who promptly published his assignment, and let that be known.

James Sanders: I am not going to be defensive and I don't think I need to be. Let me say that the Psalm Scroll [that Jim Sanders published] was a beautiful scroll, not fragments, and that makes a big difference. The complete, or more or less complete, scrolls from Cave 1 did come out in diplomatic editions (publication of photographs and maybe transcriptions). In the early days, we had that; then Cave 4 came to light with all these fragments.

Many, many inscriptions have not yet been published. More than half of the archaeological reports of excavated sites have not been published. The archaeological report concerning the excavations at Qumran has not yet been published. I was 32 years old when I unrolled the scroll, and I was told all kinds of stories. I was initiated into the fact that the Cave 4 team was largely made up of raving geniuses. They would tell about how they would meet in the museum labs, face a problem, and then discuss it at the American School later that evening and so on. It would be [J. T.] Milik who would come the next day with the solution. Milik always had a solution. He seemed to have a reputation of being a particular kind of genius; so he got all the tough stuff. And [John] Strugnell was, I think, second in line with that kind of reputation. He got the second rank of tough stuff. These are stories that I was told in the early days.

Shanks: One aspect of what Jim Sanders spoke about that may lie behind this—I really hesitate to talk about it. In a sense, it may explain why the Israelis are not pressing more vehemently for publication now that they control the scrolls. The Dead Sea Scrolls are a particularly egregious example of slow publication and this situation has caught the public imagination. But that is just the tip of the iceberg. It is a much bigger problem the profession has to face. I hope the profession will face it. I am talking now about archaeology generally. There has been reference to the fact that there is no final publication of the excavations at Qumran. I think it is being prepared now. Jean-Baptiste Humbert and another colleague are doing it. But you could go through the different nationalities that have conducted excavations in the Near East and no one would be guiltless.

The reluctance of the scholarly world to get behind the publication of the Dead Sea Scrolls or the release of the photographs may reflect this common problem and the guilt it may engender. The Dead Sea Scrolls are a particularly egregious example, because of their importance, because of the time that has elapsed and because they do not quite fit the convention: The convention that was enunciated a moment ago by Kyle McCarter that when an archaeologist excavates something, he controls the publication. He can assign it to someone else, but he controls it because he excavated it. That principle has no application here. The men who control the publication rights of the Dead Sea Scrolls did not excavate them, did not find them. Milik, who has more than he can do in a lifetime—according to Joe Fitzmyer who recently saw him, Milik is really not working anymore—he has done some marvelous work in the past and his partially complete work is very helpful, as Jim VanderKam has said, for his own work. Frank Cross is the second person. He has only one major manuscript left, the Samuel text. And John Strugnell is the third. He too has more material then he will ever be able to publish in his lifetime.

Sanders: Let's look at a positive aspect now. Gene Ulrich of Notre Dame is working very hard. We have had eight volumes in the *Discoveries in the Judaean Desert* series, which is more or less the semiofficial series in which these scrolls are published. Some are published totally outside the series. Volumes 9, 10, 11 and 12, which will all be biblical texts are all being worked on now. Gene Ulrich has oversight of them and has published in the last issue of *Revue de Qumran,* the exact listing of what scholar is charged with which books of the Bible. I think that those four volumes really have a chance of being out in 1994-1995. That would be all the biblical material.

Shanks: Let me change the subject, Jim [Sanders]. Since you mentioned the biblical manuscripts—I found your talk fascinating, especially about the pluriform traditions of the different texts—one of the simple-minded questions that lay people like myself ask is, is there any major thing about a biblical text that we did not know before that we have learned about from Qumran? One of the possibilities that comes to mind is in the Book of Samuel. There is an episode that does not quite make sense about a guy, I think his name was Nahash, who attacked some Israelites in a place called Jabesh-Gilead and said he would spare the city if he could gouge out the eyes of the Israelites. Samuel doesn't tell us why he wanted to do this, it doesn't make sense; but I think Frank Cross found a text that explains this. Does that make any sense?

VanderKam: One of the Samuel manuscripts found in Cave 4 has a reading that reflects Josephus' version of this story. When Josephus in his book, *Antiquities of the Jews,* retells the biblical story, he, of course, tells the stories in the first Book of Samuel, including the one to which Hershel was referring when Nahash, the king of the Ammonites, threatens to gouge out the right eyes of the men of Jabesh-Gilead. This, of course, gives Saul the chance to save these people. Nahash had been doing this for a while, and now he was threatening this city with the same fate. A fragment of one of the Cave 4 Samuel manuscripts indicates that Nahash had done this before and now was threatening the residents of Jabesh-Gilead. So it gives a larger context to that story. It indicates that, according to the story teller, this was not something that he had just cooked up in his mind—something with which to oppress the Jabesh-Gileadites.

Shanks: I think that, according to Frank [Cross], it was a standard practice to gouge out the eyes of rebels. Nahash had previously conquered Israelite territory, then there was a rebellion and Nahash gouged out the eyes of the Israelite rebels. But 7,000 of the rebels fled to Jabesh-Gilead so it was the eyes of this 7,000 that Nahash was after. Now, that really opens up the story. And it is not just a word that has been added or changed. It is pretty much a paragraph. Apparently, this passage fell out of the text somewhere along the line. I would like to ask Jim [Sanders], would you go so far as to restore a whole paragraph like that?

Sanders: Yes, if the canons and rules of text criticism are observed. I can't get into all that. That is too wide a field for today, but I think that it is possible. You have to be willing to do it carefully, then you are simply taking what that community understood to use in our text.

Given the enormous advances in photography since the original photographs were made, are there any plans to get new photographs of the original scrolls?

Sanders: Some of the scrolls have deteriorated and discolored badly since they were taken to Jerusalem, so that is no longer possible. Zuckerman's way of addressing the problem at the Ancient Biblical Manuscript Center involves photographing the negatives that we do have from the early days when the scrolls looked better. In some cases, as in the case of the Copper Scroll apparently, it is better to rephotograph the actual scroll. Photographic experts, like Bruce and Ken Zuckerman, would be able to determine which is better to do. I sometimes think we should do both.

I'd like to go back to the question about who put the scrolls in the caves. There apparently are some definitely sectarian documents that appear to be Essene. Are those documents mixed in with all the other documents or is there some segregation in the various caves? And could you say that some of the caves were a more general depository from Judea at that time?

VanderKam: It has been claimed that there was something like a Library of Congress classification of caves, with certain types of texts in Cave 1—specifically sectarian texts—and Greek texts in Cave 7, although that cave had very little material and most of it is too small to make out. I don't think that that works because we have copies of various books in different caves. The one I am working on—Jubilees—is an example; fragments of it were found in the first, second, third, fourth and eleventh caves. There is too much overlap between them, I think, with biblical manuscripts being found in the various caves, Psalms manuscripts and so on, and I don't know of any caves that have no sectarian documents, except the so-called small caves that yielded very, very little. I really don't think a claim like that could be made.

Shanks: Let me ask a question, Jim [VanderKam]. How do you account for the fact that you claim that these people are Essenes, but we have approximately 800 texts—admittedly most fragmentary—and "Essene" does not appear in any of them. And I would add something else! Some similar texts were found at Masada. We know that Masada was a Zealot stronghold before it was destroyed in the aftermath of the First Jewish Revolt, yet nobody claims that those documents from Masada were "Zealot" sectarian documents.

VanderKam: About the name Essene—that it has never been found. Wouldn't it be strange if these 800 manuscripts were from an Essene library and nobody bothered to mention who the people were? Well, it depends on what that word means, and nobody seems to know exactly where the word "Essene" came from. It is thought to come from a Semitic root, and there are different suggestions about its meaning: that it is the word for "pious ones," in which case it does appear; or it is a word which means "healers," which is attested in Philo for a group of people with very similar views. Another recent suggestion is that the word comes from the verb "to do" or "to make" and that these people were doers of Torah. Whether it appears at Qumran or not depends on the proper etymology, or explanation, of the word.

Some similar texts did show up at Masada, and the normal explanation has been that possibly some people from Qumran went to Masada, which is not that far away. In fact, that is the explanation that is on the sign at Qumran. Nobody knows whether that is true. I don't know that I believe it.

Are they any closer to recovering the lost books of the Bible?

Sanders: I think that Sid Leiman says there are 29 references in the Hebrew Old Testament to prior works we no longer have. We are no closer to recovering those lost books than we ever were. We don't have copies or fragments of any of them.

Shanks: There is one qualification, one speculation, that I might mention that involves the Temple Scroll. There are references in the Hebrew Bible to two lost books, books we don't have. There is nothing in the Hebrew Bible that tells you the plans for the Temple and there is a passage that indicates that the plan was given to David or Solomon. There is also a reference to another book about the laws limiting the king's prerogatives. Both of these subjects, supposedly contained in books referred to in the Bible, are treated in the Temple Scroll. Yigael Yadin has raised the possibility, not that the Temple Scroll incorporates these lost books, but that whoever wrote the Temple Scroll was somehow influenced by this and thought he was supplying this kind of loss because there are very detailed instructions and limitations on both these subjects.

Sanders: The difficulty with that is that you turn that coin over and we now, for instance, have the Prayer of Manasseh and have had for a long, long time. But the question really is, since Chronicles said that he uttered a prayer, didn't someone say that, oh well, we better fill that gap. You don't know if that's the case with the author of the Temple Scroll.

I speak as an outsider about the effect of scholarship on the practice of religion. I note from my own library that scholarship like yours has been going on for a few hundred years at least. People in the religions have been changing but not in response to your scholarship. They go their own way; and your scholarship keeps on going. But what is the point if the religionists are not going to pay attention to you?

Sanders: I think that there has been an influence, some of it good and some of it not so good. That is to say, the historic mainline churches are pretty much staffed by ministers from graduates of Harvard and Yale and Union and Claremont and so on. The graduates of these seminaries get their degrees for knowing theories about the historical formation of the Bible, but they don't know what the Bible says. This is a great lament I have. We get students now in the mainline seminaries who are ignorant of the Bible in the first place because they are not learning it at home or in church anymore. Then they come to seminary and learn all about J, E, D and P—the documentary hypothesis—but they have not read the Pentateuch yet. The documentary hypothesis is just one theory about possible formation of the Pentateuch.

George Steiner, in the *New Yorker* of February 1988, engages in a real lament and I agree with him when he says that very few people outside of theological circles, or English departments of literature know Bible content anymore. In an address that I gave at Georgetown University last year, I said, "Mr. Steiner, it is worse than you think. They don't know the Bible all that well in theological circles either." I would not want to say how much of the Bible is really known in mainline seminaries. What you get is sometimes the opposite of what you are talking about. The ministers go out into the churches and you have a gap between pulpit and pew. The guy or gal in the pulpit knows the theories about the formation of the Bible but probably hasn't read too terribly much out of 2 Chronicles recently, if ever. The people in the pew don't know it anymore either for the most part, and the minister is afraid, because the budget has to be met each fall, to tell them what he really learned about the J, E, D and P theory.

When the scrolls were first found and divvied up, no Jews were allowed to edit or publish. Why was that?

Shanks: Because the team was assembled under Jordanian auspices and that was a condition of the Jordanian government. That is not true today. I tried to stress that, when I said that this bias did not extend to the scholars themselves. This was a restriction that was imposed on them. John Strugnell, for example, who is now chief editor, has enlisted several prominent Israeli scholars—Devorah Dimant, Elisha Qimron, Emanuel Tov.

Were the caves sealed in any way? If so, I can imagine how through the years the sealing might have disintegrated, giving an opportunity for vandalism. If you had vandalism it could account for why things were mixed up in there.

McCarter: I think that a visit to the caves gives you a kind of answer. It is important to remember how inaccessible these places were, and still are. You can take a bus to Qumran now but it is still difficult to get into the 11 caves and many of the others that were found. There is almost no need, I think, for sealing up the caves.

Shanks: There is one problem and a theory: In Cave 4, the one with the 15,000 fragments of 500 different books, they were all jumbled up, and one theory is that the Roman soldiers got in there and stomped around and were responsible for a lot of the destruction.

Is there any contradiction between the Qumran texts and the text of the Hebrew Bible?

VanderKam: I do not know of anything of any significance other than maybe a word that has been dropped out of a text here and there. One interesting case is the Book of Jeremiah which was known to exist in ancient times in two different forms—a longer form and a considerably shorter form in the Greek translation of the Hebrew Bible (the Septuagint). At Qumran there has been found a Hebrew text which corresponds to the shorter Greek text of a certain section (I think it is chapter 10 of the Book of Jeremiah) which lacks certain verses that are found in the Hebrew text.

Shanks: I will take a stab at one: In Deuteronomy 32, I think, there is a reference in the Hebrew Bible to "Children of Israel" and, if you read it, "Children of Israel" does not make sense (they are dividing up the land). A fragment of this text found at Qumran does not say "Children of Israel"; it says *B'nai Elohim,* "Children of God." Now that is a little embarrassing, that the "Children of God" were divvying up the land. It does make sense in the text, but theologically it is a little rough. I believe that that corresponds to the Septuagint reading, but if you want a little embarrassment, that might suffice.

McCarter: But that last detail is important, Hershel, because it is a reading we already had; it is not a new reading at all. It simply confirms that the Greek was translated from a Hebrew text that had that reading. But we knew that reading, and I think that this is an important part of the answer to the question—a contradiction that we don't expect precisely because of the plurality of readings that comes from the time period that Professor Sanders was talking about this afternoon. The text was still fluid enough that there were many different readings and many of those have been transmitted to us either through Hebrew or Greek or some other tradition. What we are finding at Qumran is not so often a contradiction, but simply another attestation of one or another reading.

Sanders: One little point in addition to that. In text criticism we sometimes see that there have been several different solutions to a textual problem in antiquity. It may be one way in the Septuagint, another in the scrolls and still another in the Syriac translation—all of them contradictory. But they were all struggling with the same difficult text, all trying to make sense of it.